AQA Religious Studies: Ethics

A2

Exclusively endorsed by AQA

D0486931

SAINT FRANCIS XAVIER COLLEGE
MALWOOD ROAD
LONDON SW12 8EN
TELEPHONE No. 020 8772 6000
FAX No. 020 8772 6099
WEBSITE. www.sfx.ac.uk
EMAIL. enquiries@sfx.ac.uk

Robert Bowie

 Nelson Thornes

Published in 2009 by:
Nelson Thornes Ltd
Delta Place
27 Bath Road
CHELTENHAM
GL53 7TH
United Kingdom

09 10 11 12 13 / 10 9 8 7 6 5 4 3 2 1

A catalogue record for this book is available from the British Library

ISBN 978 1 4085 1383 5

Cover photograph: Getty/Stephen Johnson
Illustrations by Clinton Banbury
Page make-up by Hart McLeod

Printed and bound in Spain by GraphyCems

The authors and publisher are grateful to the following for permission to reproduce photographs and other copyright material in this book:

p16 from the film *Obedience* ©1968 by Stanley Milgram, © renewed by Alexandra Milgram, and distributed by Penn State Media Sales; p28 Python Pictures/EMI/The Kobal Collection; p33 *The Allegory of Good Government* (1338–1340) by Ambrogio Lorenzetti (c.1290–1348) from the Sala della Pace in the Palazzo Pubblico, Siena, Alinari Archive, Florence; p34 *The Allegory of Bad Government* (1338–1340) by Ambrogio Lorenzetti (c.1290–1348) from the Sala della Pace in the Palazzo Pubblico, Siena, Alinari Archive, Florence; p45 Paula Solloway/Alamy; p75 Bettmann/Corbis; p77 Andrew Leonard/Science Photo Library; p87 Fotolia; p98–9 quote from Peter Singer (ed.) *In Defence of Animals*, Oxford: Blackwell, 1985.

Every effort has been made to contact the copyright holders and we apologise if any have been overlooked. Should copyright have been unwittingly infringed in this book, the owners should contact the publishers, who will make corrections at reprint.

Contents

AQA introduction

Nelson Thornes and AQA

Nelson Thornes has worked in collaboration with AQA to ensure that this book offers you the best support for your AS or A Level course and helps you to prepare for your exams. The partnership means that you can be confident that the range of learning, teaching and assessment practice materials has been checked by the senior examining team at AQA before formal approval, and is closely matched to the requirements of your specification.

Blended learning

Printed and electronic resources are blended: this means that links between topics and activities between the book and the electronic resources help you to work in the way that best suits you, and enable extra support to be provided online. For example, you can test yourself online and feedback from the test will direct you back to the relevant parts of the book.

Electronic resources are available in a simple-to-use online platform called Nelson Thornes learning space. If your school or college has a licence to use the service, you will be given a password through which you can access the materials through any internet connection.

Icons in this book indicate where there is material online related to that topic. The following icons are used:

🔋 Learning activity

These resources include a variety of interactive and non-interactive activities to support your learning.

✅ Progress tracking

These resources include a variety of tests that you can use to check your knowledge on particular topics (Test yourself) and a range of resources that enable you to analyse and understand examination questions (On your marks …).

🔋 Research support

These resources include WebQuests, in which you are assigned a task and provided with a range of weblinks to use as source material for research.

When you see an icon, go to Nelson Thornes learning space at **www.nelsonthornes.com/aqagce**, enter your access details and select your course. The materials are arranged in the same order as the topics in the book, so you can easily find the resources you need.

How to use this book

This book covers the specification for your course and is arranged in a sequence approved by AQA.

AQA Unit 3A, Religion and Ethics, encompasses: Libertarianism, free will and determinism; Virtue ethics; Religious views on sexual behaviour and human relationships; and Science and technology.

The features in this book include:

Learning objectives

At the beginning of each section you will find a list of learning objectives that contain targets linked to the requirements of the specification.

Key terms

Terms that you will need to be able to define and understand.

Key philosophers

Key philosophers and their relevant works, listed at the beginning of some chapters.

Links

These refer you back to other parts of the book which consider similar issues.

Activity

Things for you to do that will reinforce the information you have just learned.

Take it further

Tasks for you to complete if you want to stretch your knowledge or understanding of an issue.

AQA Examiner's tip

Hints from AQA examiners to help you with your study and to prepare for your exam.

AQA Examination-style questions

Questions in the style that you can expect in your exam.

AQA examination questions are reproduced by permission of the Assessment and Qualifications Alliance.

Learning outcomes

At the end of each chapter you will find a list of learning outcomes. These remind you what you should know having completed the chapter.

Web links in the book

Because Nelson Thornes is not responsible for third-party content online, there may be some changes to this material that are beyond our control. In order for us to ensure that the links referred to in the book are as up to date and stable as possible, the websites provided are usually homepages with supporting instructions on how to reach the relevant pages if necessary.

Please let us know at **webadmin@nelsonthornes.com** if you find a link that does not work and we will do our best to correct this at reprint, or to list an alternative site.

Introduction to this book

The last century of the last millennium saw moral revolutions. The personal morality of the developed world has been challenged with radical changes to liberalise laws and attitudes on sexual relationships. Sexual activity seems to have become a leisure activity, largely disconnected from reproduction, and sexual relationships are governed only by the idea of consent. In some parts of the world gay and lesbian couples have more rights than ever before. At the same time such unions and sexual activity are criminal in other parts of the world.

Why is ethics important?

As society becomes more diverse and plural there seems to be a loss of certainty about right and wrong. Morality has become fragmented. Many moral philosophers abandoned any connection to the old morals, the old laws of religion and tradition. Some suggested that there was no way back, that morals were constructed social norms which could be dropped when human beings saw fit to do so. Some went on to challenge the idea that human beings were the freely acting creatures that they thought they were. At the same time, there are signs of a backlash; a return to a more traditional morality, especially from conservative religious cultures.

The last century also contained some of the most brutal and destructive acts against humankind that have ever been seen. During that century the combination of technology and ideology demonstrated again and again the ability for human beings to carry out large-scale, mass killings using the very latest science and technology: The Holocaust and the atomic bombing of Nagasaki and Hiroshima in the Second World War, napalm in the Vietnam war and chemical warfare in Iraq against the Marsh Arabs all stand as solemn reminders that, morally speaking, human beings seem to have a long way to go to become humane. We still apply human ingenuity and creativity in the fields of science and technology to cause destruction and death.

This book looks at these issues in four different ways. Two chapters examine the response to the challenge to moral philosophy. Chapter 1 looks at the question of whether human beings have the freedom they think, and what role freedom has in morality. Chapter 2 explores virtue ethics, a theory that challenged old arguments between deontological and teleological theories to look at the idea of morality in human development. Chapter 3 explores issues of sexual behaviour and human relationships, and Chapter 4 looks at questions of science and technology.

Tools for examining ethical theories

Here are some suggestions for questions to think about which are useful in unpacking ethical theories in particular.

We can analyse theories in an attempt to try to make sense of them. Initially we can ask, what kind of family of theories does this fit into – normative, descriptive or meta ethical? If normative, is it teleological or deontological? Does it have absolutist or relativistic tendencies?

Beyond these we can ask another set of helpful questions around the exercise of authority and judgement in the theory:

- How is the theory oriented towards moral knowledge?
- How does the theory pose the question 'What should I do?'
- How can an action be determined to be right by the theory?
- What sort of character trait does the theory uphold?
- How does the theory resolve disagreement?
- To what extent does the theory offer specific moral guidance on given acts?

You can ask these questions of an ethical theory to analyse the elements and workings of the theory in specific and applied ways. This should throw up useful pieces of information about the workings of the theory and its presuppositions, revealing areas of strength and weakness. We also can ask a number of questions to see if they seem to hold up. These are evaluative questions.

- Are any assumptions that the theory rests on true? Some theories make suggestions about human nature – are these suggestions true or can they be challenged?
- Does the theory fit together – does one thing flow from the other? Has something important been left out?
- Does the theory seem to work in practice? Is it usable as a theory?
- Does it work on its own or does it need to lean on other theories?
- Does it work well in theory but is it unmanageable in practice (or vice versa)?
- Does it only work in certain kinds of situations?

Using examples to examine ethical theories

Of course, we can use examples of situations and ethical issues to evaluate moral theories and many examples are contained in this book. Ethical examples fall into three categories:

1 Ostensive examples are taken from real life to be worked through using a theory. An example of an ostensive example would be an evaluation of the decision to drop the atom bomb on Hiroshima and Nagasaki.

2 A hypothetical example enables you to consider your decision on what to do in a plausible moral dilemma – whether to give some change to a beggar, whether using a weapon is justified in self-defence.

3 An imaginary example is an unreal scenario, such as the situation illustrated by the balloon game where you must decide to save one of the following: the Pope, a pregnant single mother or Mozart, for example.

You might like to consider which of these kinds of examples you think presents a better test for an ethical theory. When looking at the ethical examples in the book and using them to evaluate the effectiveness of an ethical theory, check to see what kind of example they are. This might help you to improve your evaluation of a theory working in practice.

1 Libertarianism, free will and determinism

By the end of this chapter you will be able to:

- identify the key elements of the debate about free will

- describe important aspects of libertarianism and determinism

- outline religious perspectives of libertarianism and determinism and make some critical judgements about them

- suggest both criticisms and strengths of libertarianism and determinism and make some judgements about the theory

- suggest implications of libertarianism and determinism.

Key terms

Hard determinists: those who maintain that all human actions are effects, caused by prior influences.

Libertarians: those who maintain that we are free to act and morally responsible for those actions.

Soft determinists: those who maintain that some human actions are determined, but that we still have moral responsibility.

Key questions

1 Are we as free as we think?
2 What factors limit our ability to act freely?
3 How should individual freedom be balanced against social interests?
4 Can we be morally *blameworthy* for our actions if we are not free?

In ethics there are three broad philosophical approaches to the ethical question of free will. **Hard determinists** maintain that all human actions are effects, caused by prior influences. Therefore, humans may not be morally blameworthy for their actions because all of their actions are determined. There are those who maintain that we are free to act and morally responsible for those actions – **libertarians**. There are those who maintain that some human actions are determined, but that we still have moral responsibility – **soft determinists**. There are also questions about what we mean by free will, with some philosophers arguing that it is possible to have a form of freedom even in a deterministic world.

The question of free will

- What if it is shown that all human actions have a cause beyond our control?

- What if the ability to make free moral choices is an illusion?

- Would we be morally responsible for our actions if they were influenced by fixed external forces?

There is an important relationship between *freedom* and *moral responsibility*. It is commonly held that we should be morally responsible for actions that we freely perform. I should be ready to accept the *blame* for the things that I freely do wrong. If I am *forced* to commit an immoral action, then I am not blameworthy. If I am forced at gunpoint to drive a getaway car from a bank robbery, then it is not my fault. Likewise, if I am

Can you be praised if you are forced to do something moral?

St Thomas Aquinas (1224–74)
Summa Theologica, 1273

St Augustine of Hippo (354–430)
Divine Election

John Calvin (1506–64) *Institutes*, 1559

David Hume (1711–76) 'Liberty', in his *An Enquiry Concerning Human Understanding*, 1748

John Locke (1632–1704) *Essay Concerning Human Understanding*, 1690

Benedict Spinoza (1632–77) *Ethica Ordine Geometrico Demonstrata* (Ethics Demonstrated with Geometrical Order), 1674

AQA Examiner's tip

Make sure that you can *explain* the differences between free will, determinism and libertarianism by using examples of both an ethical and a non-ethical nature. A non-ethical example would be reading a book; this could be an entirely free choice, or because of an exam the next day. An ethical example might be that of being brought up in a criminal household and choosing to follow in the footsteps of the family or not.

forced to commit a moral action, I am not praiseworthy. If I am forced at gunpoint to give money to charity, I am not praiseworthy. We can only attribute moral *blame* or *praise* to actions that are freely undertaken.

If, in ignorance, I perform an action that has an unpredictable immoral effect, then I am not blameworthy. If a general in a war sends his troops into a valley that he believes to be safe, he is not morally blameworthy if there is a secret ambush that kills all his troops, assuming he could not have known what was going to happen. If, on the other hand, he had sent the troops to their deaths knowingly, or without making appropriate checks, then he would be morally blameworthy. A company producing cosmetics that uses an untested chemical that causes harmful side-effects is morally responsible because it should have tested that chemical for side-effects. In instances such as these, ignorance is no excuse and negligence is immoral.

If someone is not in control of his or her actions because of drugs, alcohol or some other disorientating influence – such as an emotional trauma or a psychological condition – then that person is not entirely morally responsible for his or her actions. The drunk who kills a pedestrian may be morally blameworthy, but he has not committed as great a crime as a sober person who deliberately runs down an innocent, because the person's intention is important. If a person chooses to enter into a state of uncontrolled behaviour, such as choosing to get drunk before driving home, then that person may be more to blame than a person who unwillingly enters a disorientated state. If I kill a pedestrian because I am disorientated after someone has spiked my orange juice, I am not as responsible for my actions as the person who chooses to drink and then drive. Intention has some bearing on moral culpability. Did they mean to kill or was it an accident? Criminals who intend to commit their crimes are punished more heavily than those who commit unplanned crimes. And yet our actions do have consequences, even if we do not foresee or intend those consequences.

However, are our actions the consequence of some previous action which is beyond our control? If we can only blame or praise people for actions they freely and knowingly undertake, then it is vital that human beings have freedom to act. Morality depends on freedom. Immanuel Kant wrote: '"Ought" implies "can"'. Moral actions are freely undertaken actions.

> [I]n morals, the proper and inestimable worth of an absolutely good will consists precisely in the freedom of the principle of action from all influences
>
> *Kant, 1785*

Kant believed that humans are free to make rational choices. Without freedom, the possibility of making moral choices is denied. This ability to freely rationalise, or reason, is what sets humans apart from other animals that lack this capacity.

We cannot blame someone for not doing what they could not do. If people are not free, the possibility of making moral choices is denied. If human actions are caused by external influences, then people cannot be morally responsible for those actions. This is the challenge brought about by the idea of predestination and the determinist ethical viewpoint.

Activities

Consider these five situations:

1 A policeman, who is a poor shot, shoots dead an innocent civilian by mistake.

2 A policeman intentionally shoots dead an innocent civilian.

3 A policeman, hallucinating after taking drugs, shoots dead an innocent civilian.

4 A policeman, believing it his duty to obey the orders of the state, is commanded to shoot dead an innocent civilian and does so.

5 A policeman, threatened with execution if he does not obey orders, is commanded to shoot dead an innocent civilian and does so.

- With regard to the policeman, arrange the examples in order, from the least blameworthy to the most blameworthy.
- Is the policeman morally responsible for the death of the innocent civilian in each case?
- Should there be any difference in the way the policeman is dealt with (that is, punished)? Explain your answer.

Historically, there has been a great deal of concern over human freedom and moral responsibility.

What curtails our freedom?

Free will seems to be a really important part of being human. We think that we are different from all other living animals by virtue of the fact that we can think rationally and make moral judgements about what we should and should not do. We are not simply driven by natural urges in the way animals are. But perhaps we are not as free as we think. A number of factors may reduce our freedom quite considerably, and in some cases our belief that we are free could be an illusion.

Genetics and environment

How much are we really influenced by nature and nurture, by the genes in our system and the environment in which we live? We might think we are our own selves, free in all of our choices, but some hold that we may be far more programmed than we would like to believe, both in terms of dispositions that exist in our genetic heritage and also in our social upbringing.

In genetics we are at an early stage of understanding how much impact genetic combinations might have on our predispositions. There are frequent newspaper stories about the discovery of the 'gay gene', or the 'crime gene', but we are not yet in a position to know how much influence collections of genes might have on our behaviour and we might never be sure. There might always be variables or random elements so that while it may be more likely that a person with x genes acts in a y way, this will not translate to a cause. Nor do we fully understand how different combinations of genes might affect us. In addition, the extent to which predispositions govern our actual behaviour is not clear. In other words, I may have a biological predisposition to behave in a certain way, but I may have enough willpower to restrain my action and apply moral consideration before I act.

Take it further

Use the internet to look into scientific evidence of genetic dispositions curtailing free will.

Self-restraint and willpower

Predisposition does not necessarily lead to action. Many people are tempted to do certain things that are judged immoral, and while some do not resist temptation, others do. Self-restraint, or volition, might be found to have some genetic origin, but it might be down to other factors such as religious or ethical beliefs, or psychological or emotional capacities – inner strengths that enable us to live in a more authentic way which is closer to our principles. Perhaps some people are simply more cautious and risk averse. They would like to do the thing they are tempted to do, but are too scared of being found out.

Nevertheless there have been powerful challenges to the idea of freedom. In his book *Beyond Freedom and Dignity*, psychologist B. F. Skinner argued that much of the discussion about human moral behaviour did not take account of what science was telling us. He was particularly critical of attempts to control people by changing attitudes, building a sense of moral responsibility, or inspiring self-respect. He argued that all of these sorts of opinions have no basis in science. They do not show an understanding of the impact that the environment has on human behaviour. Skinner thought that people were fooled by an unscientific old-fashioned view of human beings that we are in control of our actions and can reason the right thing to do. Skinner believed we could have a technology of human behaviour, a way of understanding why people did the things they did. He argued that the environment was full of factors which exercised degrees of control over human beings. If Skinner is right, then our ideas about freedom and morality and also punishment are challenged.

Living in society

Individuals living together in groups form certain agreed rules of behaviour. This is often referred to as a social contract, an arrangement by which the individual gains benefits from being part of a group, at the cost of some limitations or restrictions on how the individual behaves. Freedoms and rights are given up in the interest of social order. Important here is what life would be like without such agreement. Would the law of the jungle simply apply, a free-for-all based on the survival of the fittest? Order, justice and civilisation come about, it is argued, by people agreeing to some basic rules of conduct. Within the social contract tensions can emerge over how much diversity is allowed. For instance, is the society tolerant of different religious beliefs or political opinions? Do the agreed rules affect certain groups in certain ways, such as women and their access to work and employment? People who are particularly creative or artistic, or express exotic or different ways of living, might find themselves under social pressure to change and conform, or even be forced out of the group.

Some cultures have developed profoundly mono-cultural ideas of the social contract. National Socialism in 1930s Germany expressed an idea of human beings based on racial grounds and sought to organise a racially pure state. In this view of society all those who were different were seen as threats to society, be that due to racial impurity, inappropriate gender orientation (in the case of homosexuality) or disability. Nazi Germany gives a picture of a very high level of social expectation placed on every individual by the state. The interests of the group are placed far above those of the individual and individuals must be either forced to change, contained or expelled from society.

Take it further

Use the internet to research Skinner's behaviourist psychological theory and the methods he used.

Activities

1. Do you tend to agree or disagree with Skinner? Give reasons for your view.

2. If you have a sense of resisting temptation, of wanting to do something but choosing not to do it for moral reasons, is this evidence that Skinner is wrong? Explain your answer and try to consider both viewpoints.

Activity

Some religions hold that aspects of law are wrong. For instance, some religions are pacifist and oppose war, some object to abortion and some teach that same-sex civil partnerships are wrong. Some religions permit men to take more than one wife in certain circumstances and treat men and women differently.

In what areas of life should individuals and groups of people living in a diverse society be free to live in any way they choose? What values, if any, are compulsory?

On the other hand, more **cosmopolitan** ideas of the social contract allow for degrees of diversity, difference and creativity to a degree and only restrict individual freedoms to a minimum. Groups of people may even be able to have quite significant differences in the way they go about things, such as in the case of arranged marriages, while adhering to important common values.

Conflict of free wills

Of course my freedom to act may bring me into conflict with what you want to do. Even in a situation where the state tries not to interfere in most cases, there will still be conflicts. As I walk along the pavements I may find others walking towards me. One of us will have to move if there is not to be a collision. At the supermarket I may see a particularly fresh-looking piece of wild smoked salmon and reach out for it, only to find another customer has beaten me to it. At a crossroads four approaching vehicles reach the junction at the same time. If they all proceed there will be a crash. Individual freedom requires us to think about how conflict is handled. We might place our own limits on what we do out of politeness, but it may be that such politeness expresses a social value which everyone keeps to, even if there is no actual policeman enforcing it. These societal expectations are not to be underestimated. They may be strong enough to motivate a gay man to marry a woman for the sake of the family or community.

Who should cross the junction first?

Summary of free will

In considering the question of free will we should remember:

- Moral responsibility may be mitigated by the degree to which we were free when we acted.
- Arguably environmental influences play a very strong role in determining our behaviour – perhaps we are not as free as we think!

Key terms

Cosmopolitan: accepting of groups and individuals from different cultural, ethnic and religious backgrounds within society.

Activity

Why might you argue that politeness and courtesy are essential values for a happy society?

█ We live in a diverse society where moral difference is likely to be an ongoing issue. We can either try to rule it out by expecting everyone to conform tightly to a set of principles or rules, or we can allow a degree of flexibility in society, a more cosmopolitan range of freedoms.

█ Genuine conflict is always likely to occur and we may not always be able to do the things we want to do.

█ Libertarianism

The personality and the moral self

Libertarianism is used to describe two different philosophical topics. In the philosophy of mind, libertarianism is the view that we are free and morally responsible for our actions. In political philosophy it explores the relationship between the individual and the community or state in terms of the rights and liberties that each has. Both fields have ethical implications.

An influential figure in libertarianism is John Stuart Mill (1806–73). His book *On Liberty* (1859) is an extremely important book for modern western civilisation. It contains an outspoken defence of free speech. Mill was very concerned that the individual should not be crushed by the will of the many in society or by the state. He was just as concerned that the views of the mob would crush the diversity of individual people as he was that the state would control what they did. In *On Liberty*, he wrote:

> Whatever crushes individuality is despotism, by whatever name it may be called and whether it professes to be enforcing the will of God or the injunctions of men.

Mill, 1996, p64

> In this age, the mere example of non-conformity, the mere refusal to bend the knee to custom, is itself a service.

Mill, 1996, p67

> If all mankind minus one were of one opinion, mankind would be no more justified in silencing that one person than he, if he had the power, would be justified in silencing mankind.

Mill, 1996, p19

Mill felt that the strength and value of the community and the state were provided by the value of the individuals within it. He argued:

> The worth of the state, in the long run, is the worth of the individuals composing it.

Mill, 1996, p114

and he put it another way:

> The individual is not accountable to society for his actions in so far as these concern the interests of no person but himself.

Mill, 1996, p93

Human beings have some limitations of course. People must not harm another person. He wrote:

> The only purpose for which power can be rightfully exercised over any member of a civilized community against his will is to prevent harm to others.

Mill, 1996, p13

> The liberty of the individual must be thus far limited; he must not make himself a nuisance to other people.

Mill, 1996, p56

For Mill, individuality is part of what the good life is all about. Individuality means human development. If human beings are to grow and develop they must have free speech and freedom of action within reason. Our freedom to act, freedom to be creative, marks out both our moral capacity but also our personality. So much of me is the result of the particular choices I have made. My identity is as much a feature of my own choices as it is something given at birth. Human personality is an expression of free will and human beings cannot develop if they cannot exercise their will.

Libertarians hold that moral responsibility requires freedom. They suggest we have a sense of self-determination or freedom to act. Freedom is an important, perhaps defining, feature of what it means to be a human person, what it means to be a moral self. Human beings are rational creatures with the capacity to make free moral decisions. They can weigh up different factors, give situations some thought before choosing a course of action. Libertarians are **incompatibilists** because they maintain that free will is incompatible with determinism.

Key terms

Incompatibilists: people who hold the view that free will is incompatible with determinism. Those with the view that free will is compatible with determinism are called compatibilists.

Activities

1. To what extent do you agree with Mill, that the value of a society is the sum of the value of the individuals?

2. Why do you think that Mill argues that individuality is the same as development?

3. Sometimes we think of schools as places where children are socialised, made ready for living in society, but if Mill is correct should that vision be changed and if so, what to?

Take it further

Read Mill's *On Liberty* or *The Subjection of Women* (both available online, see Further Reading and Weblinks at the end of the chapter).

Conscience

There is an idea that we should only do things we are happy about doing. We should act in a way which fits our principles and beliefs. We should act with integrity, or conscientiously. For libertarians conscience and conscientious action are extremely important. I should not be forced or required to do things that I genuinely believe to be wrong. I may hold the view that all killing is wrong and if so I should not be required to fight a war for a country, even if that country is threatened, because my own conscience would be undermined. People who hold conscience to be important see it as a central feature of human dignity; it has something to do with personal integrity. The erosion of conscience, by social pressure or direct state coercion, makes people less human because it limits our free moral decision making.

It might be argued that an individual conscience should heed to the greater will of the people, as reflected by the state for instance. However, this view gives no value to the integrity of individuals and minorities. It gives value only to the weight of the majority. There is also a sense that when a human being is forced to act against his or her will, a crime is done against all human beings, not simply the individual. It is a crime against the very idea of the human person. This is not an argument for total freedom of the individual but, rather, a reminder that the community cannot make a claim on an individual that totally diminishes that individual. It may have been in the majority interests of Nazi Germany to eliminate Jews and others who were seen as impure, but such acts are still wrong.

Religion and conscience

Religion and conscience have often been associated with one another. While there is no word for conscience in Hebrew, conscience does play a part in many of the stories in the Bible. Jonathan Gorsky (1999) argues that this can be seen in stories such as when Joseph was tempted by the wife of Potiphar (Genesis 39:8). Joseph resisted and a rabbinic commentary suggests he was about to succumb when conscience presented itself as his father's face. Elsewhere there are accounts of how sinful acts left the sinner with a profound sense of sin in the heart (2 Samuel 24:10). This prompting of the heart is an indicator of conscience although it does not necessarily point in the right direction. Rabbinic literature discusses the existence of both evil and good inclinations. Good inclinations are supported by the Torah and reason. However, Gorsky notes that there seem to be tensions and conflicts with the traditional sources when it comes to matters of conscience, suggested for instance by the role of women in those sources.

Ron Geaves (1999) suggests that in Islam an understanding of the centrality of revelation is essential for understanding the role of conscience. Islam means surrendering to the will of Allah, so any idea of an individual internal moral authority is alien to Islam. What is more, inner workings of conscience cannot be relied upon. However, the social dimension of conscience is found within Islam in the idea of the Ummah, the Muslim community, as the place where Islamic law is lived out. An exception to this is from within the Sufi tradition where there is a sense of an individual awareness of conscience as the soul must be held ready for the grace of illumination experienced in the heart.

In the New Testament, St Paul mentions conscience many times. He describes it as an awareness of what is good and bad, and observes that it can be weak and mistaken (1 Corinthians 8:10–12). Christian writers in the first few centuries developed explanations of conscience and its role in moral decision making. St Jerome (c.340–420 CE) saw conscience as the power to distinguish good from evil, writing 'the spark of conscience … with which we discern that we sin' (Potts, 1980).

St Augustine of Hippo (334–430 CE) considered conscience to be a tool for observing the law of God within human hearts: 'men see the moral rules written in the book of light which is called Truth from which all laws are copied' (De Trinitate, sections 14, 15, 21). God gives us conscience to determine his law, which is laid down. St Augustine identified conscience as the *voice of God* speaking to us, which we must seek within ourselves. This intuitive activity reveals the most God-like behaviour, so bringing us into close unity with God.

AQA Examiner's tip

If the question does not ask you to give a typical example of your answers from religion, do not feel that you have to. Look at the rest of the question; there will probably be a request to put religious examples in elsewhere. If you add religious examples too early, you will have nothing else new to say and will end up repeating yourself.

■ Activities

Consider the following definitions of conscience. Choose one which you find most plausible and justify your choice.

■ 'Knowledge within oneself', 'The faculty or principle which pronounces upon the moral quality of one's actions or motives, approving the right and condemning the wrong.' (*Oxford English Dictionary*)

■ 'Conscience is thus ... the voice of our true selves which summons us ... to live productively, to develop fully and harmoniously. It is the guardian of our integrity.' (*Fromm, 1947*)

■ 'It is the reason making moral judgements or choice values.' (*St Thomas Aquinas, 1274*)

■ 'The built in monitor of moral action or choice values.' (*John Macquarrie, in Bowie, 2001*)

Aquinas

Conscience is thought of in different ways. Some argue it is the voice of God, the way in which profound truths are conveyed to us. Others see it more as a faculty, a system by which we make moral decisions. St Thomas Aquinas is an example of the latter. He saw conscience as a device or faculty for distinguishing right from wrong rather than an inner knowledge. He thought that people basically tended towards the good and away from evil (the 'synderesis rule'). Working out what the good things and evil things were was the main problem. Aquinas thought that the reason people sometimes did evil deeds was because they had made a mistake. They had pursued an apparent good and not a real good – their consciences were mistaken. Aquinas writes:

> If a mistaken reason bids a man to sleep with another man's wife, to do this will be evil based on ignorance of divine law he ought to know; but if the misjudgment is occasioned by thinking the woman really is his own wife and she wants him then his will is free from fault.

Aquinas, 1274

Rather than being a voice that commands one thing or another, conscience is 'reason making right decisions' (Aquinas, *Summa Theologica*, I–II, I). In other words, conscience deliberates between good and bad. There are two elements of the process of making moral decisions. *Synderesis* is right reason, the awareness of the moral principle to do good and avoid evil. *Conscientia* distinguishes between right and wrong and makes the moral decision.

Butler

Joseph Butler was an Anglican priest and theologian. He saw conscience as the final moral decision-maker:

> There is a principle of reflection in men by which they distinguish between approval and disapproval of their own actions ... this principle in man ... is conscience

Butler, 1726

Butler believed that humans were influenced by two basic principles, *self-love* and *benevolence* (love of others). Conscience directs us towards focusing on the happiness or interest of others and away from focusing on ourselves.

Like Aquinas, Butler held that conscience could both determine and judge the rightness and wrongness of actions. However, Butler went on to state that conscience comes into play in situations without any introspection and has the ultimate authority in ethical judgements. For Butler, conscience gives us instant intuitive judgements about what we should do. He wrote:

> Had it strength as it has right; had it power as it had manifest authority, it would absolutely govern the world.

Butler, 1726

Butler identified conscience as a guide that God has given us in our human nature. It is our guide to moral behaviour and must be obeyed. The fact that your conscience instructs you to act in a certain way is adequate justification to behave in that way. You should not even consider alternatives. If your conscience commands, you must obey unquestioningly. This is a far more intuitive view of conscience than Aquinas' account:

> But allowing that mankind hath the rule of right within himself, yet it may be asked, 'What obligations are we under to attend to and follow it?' … Conscience does not only offer itself to show us the way we should walk in, but it likewise carries its own authority with it, that it is our natural guide, the guide assigned us by the Author of our nature; it therefore belongs to our condition of being, it is our duty to walk in that path, and follow this guide without looking about to see whether we may not possibly forsake them with impunity.

Butler, 1726

Butler gives intuitive moral judgements of conscience absolute authority and this is questionable. Surely it is at least possible that consciences could be misled or simply misinformed, and so could err. An intuitive conscience, which is obeyed unquestioningly, could be used to justify all sorts of acts. For this reason, Catholic Christianity has tended towards Aquinas' position, which gives weight to conscience but allows for the possibility of error where conscience directs a person to go against the law of God through ignorance.

Conscience as a moral guide?

St Paul believed that conscience was within the centre of the soul:

> They can demonstrate the effects of the law engraved on their hearts, to which their own conscience bears witness

Romans 2:15

Acting on your conscience is acting on your innermost convictions and involves an act of integrity. St Jerome thought it the capacity to make judgements, and a power of the soul. The Roman Catholic Church adopted Aquinas' understanding that not following conscience was always wrong. It is a deep sense of right and wrong from God, although He also taught that conscience can never motivate you to do something that goes against what is morally right (as determined by natural law). Aquinas believed that consciences should be informed, as ignorance can lead conscience astray.

The Catholic cardinal John Henry Newman (1801–90) took what seems a more intuitionist approach to conscience. Newman believed that to follow conscience is to follow a divine law as it is a messenger from God. Newman was a devout Catholic, but the quote 'I toast the Pope, but I toast conscience first' is attributed to him. Ultimately, the Roman Catholic Church's teaching on conscience reflects both Newman and Aquinas, maintaining that conscience is the law that speaks to the heart: 'a law written by God' (Pastoral Constitution, *Gaudium et Spes*, 1965). Obedience to conscience sustains human dignity, and human beings are judged by it.

Today, Catholics are encouraged to *inform* their consciences before acting on them. In *Dignitatis Humanea, the Declaration on Religious Liberty* (1965), the Vatican Council said:

> All are bound to follow their conscience faithfully in every sphere of activity so that they may come to God, who is their last end. Therefore, the individual must not be forced to act against conscience nor be prevented from acting according to conscience, especially in religious matters.

Flannery, 1996, Chapters 1, 3

However, there is disagreement about what you should do when your informed conscience goes against the established teaching of the Church. In principle, this should be impossible, but many Catholics have difficulty in accepting certain aspects of the Church's sexual teachings. Some research suggests the teaching on the use of artificial contraception is widely ignored – Catholics are prepared to ignore it on the basis of conscience. The Church teaches that it is intrinsically wrong to use artificial methods of contraception, but the experience of many Catholic couples brings them into disagreement with this teaching.

Conscience preventing free will

Sigmund Freud (1856–1939) believed that at its most fundamental the human psyche was inspired by powerful instinctive desires that had to be satisfied. However, children quickly learn that the world restricts the degree to which these desires are satisfied. Humans create the *ego*, which takes account of the realities of the world and society. A 'super-ego' internalises and reflects anger and disapproval of others. A guilty conscience is created, which grows into a life and power of its own irrespective of the rational thought and reflection of the individual. This conscience is pre-rational. Rather, it is the inevitable outcome of conflict and aggression. Conscience can then become a force to curtail our behaviour and limit our freedom.

Psychologists since Freud have amended Freud's theory. They suggest an explanation in terms of a mature and immature conscience. The mature and healthy conscience can be identified with the ego's reflection about the best way of achieving integrity. It can be characterised as something that is concerned with what is right and wrong, and that acts on things of value. It looks out to the world, developing new insights into situations. The mature conscience is dynamic, responsive and focused on the future.

The immature conscience (super-ego) can be identified with the mass of feelings of guilt that have been put there at an early pre-rational stage by parents, schooling, and so on. It may inspire actions simply to gain approval. It is concerned with feelings and it blindly obeys. It is backward-looking and the amount of guilt has little to do with the importance of the action.

These two consciences may conflict. I may feel guilty about going shopping on a Sunday, because it was instilled in me as a child that this was wrong, although I no longer believe that it is wrong. The super-ego reflects human social nature. We belong to a group and our life depends on our relationship with others. The group imposes controls over our desires, and in this way harmony can be achieved and society can survive. The mature conscience, on the other hand, is the expression of an individual search for self-fulfilment. It claims autonomy over social pressures. The individual is not content to do what everyone else does and be part of the crowd.

This psychological account of conscience is a recent explanation which can challenge the use of conscience to justify free will. It points to a possibility that we are more restricted in our actions because of conscience or, more accurately, guilt.

Which would you listen to?

Key terms

Causally undetermined: when a moral choice is made, there is no overriding power making the person choose one or another.

The causally undetermined choice

For libertarians what matters is that choices are **causally undetermined**. They genuinely choose, themselves, what to do.

David Hume (1711–76) described liberty in his *An Enquiry Concerning Human Understanding* (1748):

Activities

1. What is meant by conscience? Give three different accounts.

2. What factors might influence the formation of conscience?

3. Why could it be argued that we have a duty to follow our consciences, and what could be said against that claim?

4. When, if ever, is it right to go against your conscience?

5. Under what circumstances might it be morally permissible to break the laws of the state to follow your conscience?

6. What factors might make our conscience an unreliable guide?

7. Can you suggest some reasons for believing that conscience is a reliable moral guide?

8. In what ways do philosophers argue that conscience is linked to God?

9. What arguments might challenge a link between conscience and God or anything religious?

10. What are the strengths and weaknesses of the arguments that conscience is linked to right reason (Aquinas), intuition (Butler) or guilt (Freud)?

By liberty, then, we can only mean a power of acting or not acting, according to the determinations of the will; that is, if we choose to remain at rest, we may; if we choose to move, we also may.

Hume, 1748, Section 8, Part 1, paragraph 73

Libertarians believe that we are free to act, and morally responsible for those actions. They believe that we are not compelled to act by forces outside our moral consciousness. Moral actions are not chance or random events, but result from the values and character of the moral agent.

We have an idea that when we act we are choosing our actions. We perceive ourselves as free agents, capable of making moral choices and responsible for those choices. Humans have a sense of decision making. Sometimes we are torn between two options, both of which we feel equally uncertain about and we deliberate before making a decision. C. A. Campbell (1976) writes:

Here, and here alone, so far as I can see, in the act of deciding whether to put forth or withhold the moral effort required to resist temptation and rise to duty, is to be found an act which is free in the sense required for moral responsibility; an act of which the self is sole author, and of which it is true to say that 'it could be' (or, after the event, 'could have been') otherwise

Campbell, 1976

The pool ball is hit by the cue and moves across the table. While humans are constrained by the laws of physics, they are not like the ball in moral behaviour. If I stub my toe against a rock, I will feel pain. In my moral behaviour I am autonomous. If I am brought up among criminals I may be predisposed to think that stealing is acceptable, but moral perception can present the idea that it is wrong. Some people give in to temptation while others hold out.

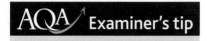

Examiner's tip

It may sound obvious, but make sure you have a clear understanding of the difference between libertarianism, free will and (hard and soft) determinism. Many candidates *think* they know the difference, but in the exam they come unstuck because they have not separated out the definitions in their own minds. Create your own definitions on different-coloured sticky notes.

■ Activities

1 Can you think of examples in your life or the life of others, of seemingly free choices made in the past which may in fact have external causes?

2 In the 1990s, a group of Liverpool women broke into a British Aerospace factory and attacked a number of Hawk trainers that were to be delivered to Indonesia. They committed trespass and did criminal damage costing thousands of pounds. They accused British Aerospace of aiding and abetting the murder of civilians in East Timor. They maintained that the planes, which experts say can carry machine guns or light bombs for ground assault, had been used to attack the civilians. The jury found the four women not guilty of damaging a jet fighter, although they admitted striking one plane with a hammer.

a Was the jury's decision correct?

b Is it ever right to take the law into your own hands in a civilised society, or should the courts always be used to pursue grievances?

c If an anti-abortionist was to destroy an abortion clinic, so preventing abortions – which were murder in his or her eyes – should he or she be prosecuted and, if so, on what basis?

3 Approximately 145,000 Jehovah's Witnesses live in the UK and the Republic of Ireland. Many refuse to consent to blood transfusions due to passages in the Bible that forbid the consumption of someone else's blood. In the event that a child of a Jehovah's Witness couple needs a blood transfusion, doctors may overrule the wishes of the parents and the child not to allow it. Should doctors or courts have the power to overrule parents and children who believe that the child's immortal soul would be in peril if such a procedure were to go ahead?

■ Determinism

There once was a man who said damn!
It is borne in upon me I am
An engine that moves
In predestinate grooves;
I'm not even a bus, I'm a tram.

Maurice Hare (1886–1967)

■ Activities

A schoolgirl attacks another girl in the playground for no apparent reason, seriously injuring her. The girls have never met before and do not know each other.

1 Did the attacker act freely?

2 What factors might we want to consider in deciding the extent to which her action was free or determined?

3 How might the attacker's behaviour have been influenced by deterministic factors?

The principle of causality and hard determinism

Libertarianism is based on a principle that says we are free to make choices. However, we have seen in this chapter that there are those who doubt that freedom really exists. It is possible that our belief that we have freedom to act is misplaced. Benedict Spinoza was suspicious about our belief that we are free and thought we were ignorant of the real causes behind our actions.

An infant thinks it freely seeks milk, an angry child thinks that it freely desired vengeance, or a timid child thinks it freely chooses flight. Again, a drunken man thinks that he speaks by the free decision of the mind those things which, if he were sober, he would keep to himself. ... So experience teaches as clearly as reason that men think themselves free on account of this alone, that they are conscious of their actions and ignorant of the causes of them.

Spinoza, 1674

Hard determinism is the view we are not free and cannot be held morally responsible for our actions:

And the first Morning of Creation wrote
What the Last Dawn of Reckoning shall read.

Khayyam, 1120

Pear trees cannot bear bananas. The instincts of a spaniel cannot be the instincts of an ostrich. Everything is planned, connected, limited.

Voltaire, 1764

Ted Honderich defines hard determinism as the view that 'all our choices, decisions, intentions, other mental events, and our actions are no more than effects of other equally necessitated events' (Honderich, 1995, p194). All actions have a prior cause. Humans are not free to act. Our actions are determined by a complex set of prior causes. It is as if we are trams, running along fixed rails. Determinism sometimes draws on the Newtonian view that all physical objects, living or otherwise, must exist in accordance with natural laws.

Internal and external causation

Are there biological causes to our behaviour or external environmental ones?

Genetics may have a powerful influence on how we respond. Our socio-economic backgrounds, religio-cultural backgrounds and experience of life may affect us in such a way that our behaviour is determined rather than free. While few scientists would argue that genes cause people to do things, the combinations of all these elements might. In 2002 scientists found evidence that a particular gene predisposed children towards bad behaviour and they concluded that children who were abused and had the gene were more likely to go on to abuse others.

Clarence Darrow was an American attorney who defended two boys who murdered a 14-year-old called Bobby Franks. The two murderers were rich and very intelligent, and had planned a perfect crime to illustrate their superiority over society. They were brought to trial facing the death penalty, but Darrow argued successfully for their sentence to be commuted to life imprisonment because the boys were products of their upbringing. Darrow thought that criminals should still be sent to prison to protect society, but argued in court that it should not be assumed that they are responsible for their actions.

AQA Examiner's tip

When explaining the 'causes' of hard determinism, do not just list them. Show the examiner that you understand why psychology, genetics, natural law, etc. could be seen as causes of hard determinism. Do this by giving brief explanations of what each term means and then an equally brief example of the same, showing all the time how it relates to determinism.

Take it further

Use the internet to find out more information about the Darrow case.

Activity

A boy suffers from abuse at the hands of his father who is drunk and violent much of the time. The boy develops a drug habit and at school exhibits antisocial behaviour, causing discipline difficulties in the classroom and bullying other children.

To what extent can the boy be held morally responsible for his actions?

Activity

Darrow believed the boys he represented were products of society but should still go to prison. How does this argument affect the relationship between freedom and morality?

Milgram's experiments on obedience to authority

Take it further

Use the internet to undertake further research into the Eichmann trial and the Milgram experiments.

These examples lend weight to the hard determinists' cause. If our actions are truly determined, then in what sense can we be morally responsible for them? Is it fair to punish people for committing actions beyond their control? The law considers people who have limited control over their actions because of extreme psychological or emotional difficulties as having 'diminished responsibility'. The emotionally distraught and beaten wife who kills her husband is not acting with total moral freedom. Her emotional state has distorted her judgement and she may have felt driven to an extreme which presented itself to her as the only way out. She is treated differently in court from the cold, calculating killer. But what if we all suffer from diminished responsibility, because all of our actions are determined by prior causes?

Freedoms may also be limited by the community, society or authority. The majority may bear down on the minority so that minorities either become like the majority or are expelled from the group. On the other hand, there may be internal causes for our actions, predispositions built up through exposure to the environment in which we live.

A series of experiments published by Yale University Psychologist Stanley Milgram in 1963 suggested that ordinary people could be persuaded to carry out acts of cruelty with little more than a strong authority figure asking them to do so. The experiments were carried out after the trial of Nazi war criminal Adolf Eichmann in Jerusalem, who gave at his court trial the excuse of following orders for his role in the Holocaust. In the experiment, two actors would pretend to be a scientist on the one hand and a volunteer tied to a chair apparently linked to electric currents. Genuine volunteers were asked to participate in a memory test experiment. They had to deliver electric shocks to the actor-volunteer in the chair at the behest of the actor-scientist. In reality there were no shocks. The real experiment was to test whether ordinary people would, simply at the behest of a figure of authority, do unpleasant things, lending support to Eichmann's excuse and also Skinner's argument. Milgram argues that the experiments demonstrated that ordinary people would do evil things if asked to do so by an authority figure. This lends weight to the determinist argument that our moral freedom is illusory and open to manipulation by external environmental factors.

Activities

1. How convincing were Milgram's experiments that our behaviour is or can be controlled by external factors? Justify your answer.

2. To what extent is our behaviour controlled by other factors? Which factors present a controlling influence?

3. To what extent are our actions predictable? If our actions are unpredictable, does this undermine the determinist's argument?

Soft determinism

The free-will–determinism debate can be seen in black-and-white terms, as one thing or the other. However, there is a lot of middle ground.

Soft determinism holds that only some aspects of human beings are determined, and therefore we are morally responsible for our actions. Soft determinists argue that determinism does not rule out free will. They believe that certain elements of determinism and free will are compatible. For them, freedom to act is acting voluntarily and not out of coercion.

An act is free unless compelled by another person. This midway position suggests that some of our actions are conditioned, while others have so complex a collection of causes that they may properly be described as freely decided or willed.

A soft determinist will argue that our actions might be hypothetically free. That is to say, were our upbringing and resulting psychology a little different, an alternative choice could have been made. Free will does not mean without any influence. Hume believed that free acts are not uncaused. Instead they are caused by our choices and our choices are determined by our beliefs, desires and our personalities. Our decisions are made as a part of a process that has a causal chain of events and so are determined.

It is possible to change our behaviours. So for instance, if I suffer from anxiety attacks due to an association I make in some situations with an event in my past, by receiving counselling and psychiatric help, I may prevent the trigger for the panic attack occurring in future.

Soft determinists are criticised by hard determinists for failing to realise the extent to which human freedom is limited, and by libertarians for failing to realise the true extent of human freedom. Libertarians will argue that what soft determinists call free choice is not free choice but something else. However, soft determinists think that libertarians do not fully understand the significance of human psychology and that free choices cannot be undetermined causes. However, a line still has to be drawn between that which is determined and that which is open to choice. I might do something because of my beliefs and values, or I might do something because of an uncontrolled compulsion which I have. I may have had some choice in the development of my character, or had no choice at all. Perhaps I have been distorted by powerful personal difficulties which have affected the way I think and act in negative ways. Are these the same sorts of thing? Soft determinists have to agree on precisely what is and what is not a determining factor and clarify what makes things not free. The complexities of physics, genetics and psychology make such a line difficult for them to draw.

Religious perspectives on libertarianism and determinism

Religious perspectives on the question of free will and the theories of libertarianism and determinism vary significantly.

The traditional Judeo-Christian view is that human beings are free, autonomous agents, responsible for their actions. In Genesis, Adam and Eve exercise free will in choosing to eat the forbidden fruit. They are held responsible for their actions by God, who punishes them. St Thomas Aquinas, the Christian theologian and philosopher, wrote, 'man chooses not of necessity but freely' (*Summa Theologica* (1274), 1 PT 1, qu 13 a 6). The main Christian denominations believe that we are free to choose to do good or sin. For some traditions this has led to the views about conscience considered above.

However, there is an alternative view in Christian writings which was and is held by some Protestant Churches. This is the view that God has already decided who will be saved and who will not. This idea, which originates in St Paul's letter to the Romans, is called **predestination**:

Activity

Make a list of possible factors that influence an individual (for instance religion, family, genes, etc.). For each factor, try to decide to what extent the factor is an influencing factor or a determining factor. In cases where you think a factor could be influencing or determining depending on the situation or degree, try to define the difference in degree.

AQA Examiner's tip

When it comes to looking at determinism within a religion, make sure that you are aware of arguments from both sides, i.e. that there are deterministic and libertarian interpretations within all religions. Be confident that you are able to explain why both interpretations are held within a faith and how adherents got their views; be able to quote confidently from scripture and/or institutional teachings.

Key terms

Predestination: the view that God has already decided who will be saved and who will not.

> And we know that in all things God works for the good of those who love him, who have been called according to his purpose. For those God foreknew he also predestined to be conformed to the likeness of his Son, that he might be the firstborn among many brothers. And those he predestined, he also called; those he called, he also justified; those he justified, he also glorified.

Romans 8:28–30 (New International Bible)

Augustine's writing on the Divine Election suggests predestination:

> The potter has authority over the clay from the same lump to make one vessel for honour and another for contempt.

Augustine, Sermon 26 xii, 13

The Protestant reformer John Calvin described predestination as:

> the eternal decree of God, by which he determined that he wished to make of every man. For he does not create everyone in the same condition, but ordains eternal life for some and eternal damnation for others

Calvin, 1559, in McGrath, 1994

The idea that God decides who receives salvation and who does not at creation suggests that humans do not have free will with regard to their moral or religious behaviour. This idea has significance in the debate about whether human beings save themselves by their actions or whether they are saved by God's grace alone. However, any predetermination that I am to be saved by God's Grace does not, in and of itself, necessarily prevent our free will. We still may be able to make free choices.

St Thomas Aquinas argued that since the fall of man, man was stained by original sin. This is a loss of the righteousness that humanity had before the fall. This came about because man went against his nature by sinning in the Garden of Eden. Human nature has been impaired by human sin and is in need of redemption. While this does not prevent free moral action, it suggests a weakening in the moral fabric of humanity that needs to be repaired through restoration that only God can bring.

Within Islam there is also a strong sense that what happens occurs because it is God's will that it should be. Nothing can happen without it being in accordance with God's will. This seems closer to the deterministic view that all actions have causes, but it is not quite the same. God does not force every drop of rain to fall, even though rain falls in accordance with His will. However, in Islam there is a clear idea that a human being has a duty to act as God's regent on earth, to make appropriate moral decisions and so on. In other words, while there is this sense that all things happen only in accordance with God's will, there is also this important role that human beings have as agents of God and therefore they have the capacity to act freely, following their duty to do so.

Within Hinduism, Buddhism and Sikhism the role of causality has particular associations around the doctrine of karma. Human actions cause effects that are felt in the next life. Things experienced in this life are the effects of actions carried out in the previous life. Karma is not a punishment or reward but a consequence of an action. It may be that a person who wants to do good cannot do good and in these situations the intention has karmic force. Freedom may be limited by the consequences of previous actions in previous lives. However, human beings do have some freedom to act in the present life, much more than other creatures. They still have choices which they may make. The human life is the life in which it is possible for human beings to do that which is right. Free action is important if the cycle of rebirth can be broken through doing good and creating good karma or acquiring merit.

Hard determinism challenges the possibility for the religious to lead the good life. While some religions have traditions of predetermination within them and even elements of fate, for the most part human freedom to do good, to turn to God, for instance, seems important. At the same time libertarianism, as the individual's right to do whatever he or she chooses to do, does not fit the idea that religions have within them moral codes which should be followed.

 ## Issues arising

How free are human actions and choices?

We operate on a working theory that we choose what to do. We are thinking, evaluating human beings with the power to act. It is a central characteristic and capacity of what it means to be a human being. However, there are many influences which might restrict our actions and choices, some that we are aware of and others which we are not aware of. Firstly then, how we think about moral choices, the ideas, beliefs and values which we have adopted or been bought up with, all come to bear. When faced with a choice to do something I want to do but think may be bad, the ways of thinking which have been engrained in me will put pressure on my will. I may feel anxious about doing wrong simply because I am scared to act. I may see the act as risky and be averse to taking such a risk. I may be predisposed to behave in certain ways which I am not even conscious of. My psychological profile may mean I am simply very unlikely to act in a certain way. It is very difficult to get an objective view on the way in which different forces come to bear on us when we try to make a decision. We may be much less free than we think, and we may not be in a position to know how free that is.

Can you have true libertarianism?

An extreme extension of libertarianism is that a human being should be completely free to act and the presence of others impairs that freedom. Put another way, the presence of more than one person brings about conflict of free wills. If I have to take account of anyone else or obey anyone else when deciding what to do, then my liberty is curtailed. However, even in isolation it is arguable that we should not treat our actions as if they had no moral consequences. Libertarianism has always deployed the harm principle to curtail human action. If there were absolutely no constraints on anyone no one could be free because of what others would do.

Libertarianism does not advocate anarchy or antinomianism. Advocates of libertarianism essentially argue that the individual person has a value which is measured in terms of their distinctiveness and creativity rather than the extent to which they fit in with others. It limits and clarifies the occasions when freedom should be restricted. Rather than starting from a perspective that says 'What should we allow people to do?', libertarianism starts from the perspective of saying 'What, if any, limits should we place on people's freedom?'.

Does libertarianism require no influences to be truly free?

It seems impossible to imagine that there are no influences on us. Our social upbringing, family traditions, culture and society all must have some influence on the way we think and act. Does this mean we are not truly free? Is this what libertarianism expects?

If by true freedom we mean we act completely disconnectedly from anything else, any other experience or thought system, any other perceptions or beliefs, then we are not truly free. However, this is not the kind of freedom that libertarianism advocates. Robert Kane argued that we may have many character traits which have developed in our life experience, but these may have formed indeterministically, in self-forming actions. Our actions may flow from our character, and yet are still free from determinism (Kane, 2003).

Can we be held responsible for our actions?

It seems reasonable to argue that if we cannot choose how to behave we should not be held responsible for our actions. Morality seems to require freedom, and Kant and other moral philosophers believed the two were related. If then a strong case is made against the possibility of freedom, whether from an argument of internal or external causation, is there any justification for still holding people accountable for their actions?

Libertarians would certainly argue that freedom and moral responsibility are linked, and hard determinists are likely to argue that indeed we are not at all free so people are not individually responsible. Hard determinists might hold that a person should be held responsible by society, even if they have not individually willed the actions they are now held responsible for. A case could be made for there to be some sense of justice in society; a need to hold people to account. Nevertheless there is something uncomfortable about detaching free will from moral culpability.

Soft determinists would argue that it is possible to hold both a lack of freedom and responsibility, because the kind of freedom which people have is not uncaused free will. In other words there is still a possibility of change and some degree of responsibility. An action may be caused by something prior but does not strip all responsibility away from the individual.

Strengths and weaknesses for making ethical choices

An important argument for libertarianism is the human sense of decision making. While we have a sense of freedom, a sense of deliberating over our options, determinists maintain this is an illusion of freedom. Benedict Spinoza (1632–77) wrote:

> men think themselves free on account of this alone, that they are conscious of their actions and ignorant of the causes of them

Spinoza, 1674

John Locke (1632–1704) illustrates the view with the idea of a sleeping man who is moved into a locked room. He wakes and chooses not to try to leave the room. He believes that he could leave the room by walking through the door, while in fact the door is locked and he could never do it. We may believe that we have free will and we may feel that we can choose any number of options, when in truth our moral choices are determined by factors beyond our control. Perhaps we spend a long time deliberating over the possible choices; perhaps we feel unsure what to do. In the end, we make a decision, believing that we have freely done so. Determinists hold that in actual fact it was inevitable that we would come to this decision because of the background causes.

Libertarianism does not explain human action, yet surely our actions are caused or can be explained by something? Libertarianism attributes our moral judgement to an objective source, unaffected by environment or upbringing, but this is questionable. Surely human motives are subject to influence from many factors which at the very least leave us in a soft determinist position.

Hard determinism has a number of profound consequences. It casts doubt on our hopes for the future and how we consider the morality of others. Determinism means that we are mistaken to praise some people for being good or to blame others for being bad. In addition, if our actions are determined, then we cannot deliberate rationally. The idea that we make choices ourselves and that we decide what to do is illusory. The whole notion of moral responsibility is called into question. Murderers murder because they have the wrong genes, poor upbringing, poor parents or poor teachers. This impacts on notions of punishment. It seems wrong to punish people for acting immorally if they are not responsible for their actions. In the following card-playing example the loser cannot be blamed for losing.

> For example, if poker-playing Diamond Jim, who is holding only two pairs, has no power over the fact that Calamity Sam draws a straight flush, and if a straight flush beats two pairs (and assuming Jim has no power to alter this fact), then it follows that Jim has no power over the fact that Sam's straight flush beats Jim's two pairs.

McKenna, 2004

Jim cannot change the cards he has or the cards the other player has. He does not have freedom, and he cannot be blamed for losing. In a world without freedom, responsibility also goes. Freedom and determinism seem incompatible.

Because of this pessimistic vision of the implications of determinism, some prefer soft determinism. The philosopher William James, used the phrase 'soft determinist' in his essay *The Dilemma of Determinism* (James, 2005). He argued that it was not so much an issue of personal responsibility but one of hope. Hard determinism could lead to pessimism or a terrible subjective moral judgement. Some space must be left for chance in actions, rather than free will. Chance has some influence in human action so there is some hope.

Arguments have been made by those who think determinism and moral responsibility are compatible and they work by developing a different sense of what it means to be free. Honderich gives the following example of this argument:

> Polly is faced with a decision between doing the right thing or simply indulging a selfish desire. Polly, being the person she is, decides to do the right thing. As a matter of fact, even if she had been about to decide to be selfish, she would have decided to do the right thing. This is because there is also a demon neuroscientist in the story. He has implanted a device in her brain such that if she were to be about to decide to do the selfish thing, she would instead decide on the right thing.

Honderich, 2002

■ **Activities**

1 What is meant by the phrase '"ought" implies "can"'?

2 What is the relationship between freedom and moral responsibility?

3 Outline two religious views of human freedom?

4 Explain the differences between hard determinism, soft determinism and libertarianism. Critically evaluate each view.

Polly can be credited with doing a good thing, even though determinism is true. She made a decision that was the kind of thing she would have done anyway. She was not compelled to make the decision. In this perspective, freedom and determinism are compatible.

However, whether the kind of free will being described is the kind of free will libertarians believe in is far from clear.

■ Extracts from key texts

Aristotle

Actions are commonly regarded as involuntary when they are performed (a) under compulsion, (b) as the result of ignorance. An act, it is thought, is done under compulsion when it originates in some external cause of such a nature that the agent or person subject to the compulsion contributes nothing to it. Such a situation is created, for example, when a sea captain is carried out of his course by a contrary wind or by men who have got him in their power. But the case is not always so clear … An involuntary act being one performed under compulsion or as the result of ignorance, a voluntary act would seem to be one of which the origin or efficient cause lies in the agent, he knowing the particular circumstances in which he is acting.

Aristotle, 350 BCE

Pierre Laplace

Laplace was an 18th-century French physicist and mathematician.

An intelligence knowing all the forces acting in the nature at a given instant … would be able to comprehend in one single formula the motions of the largest bodies as well as the lightest atoms in the world, provided that its intellect were sufficiently powerful to subject all data to analysis; to it nothing would be uncertain, the future as well as the past would be present to its eyes.

Laplace, 1820

A. J. Ayer

Either it is an accident that I choose to act as I do or it is not. If it is an accident, then it is merely a matter of chance that I did not choose otherwise; and if it is merely a matter of chance that I did not choose otherwise, it is surely irrational to hold me morally responsible for choosing as I did. But if it is not an accident that I choose to do one thing rather than another, then presumably there is some causal explanation of my choice: and in that case we are led back to determinism.

Ayer, 1954

Frances S. Collins, M.D., Ph.D., Director, National Center for Human Genome Research

As genetic predispositions to everything from cancer or diabetes to novelty-seeking behaviour or homosexuality are being reported almost daily in the scientific literature (and regrettably often overstated in the popular press), a new and dangerous brand of genetic determinism is subtly invading our culture. Carried to its extreme, this 'Genes R Us' mentality would deny the value of social interventions to maximize individual potential, destabilize many of our institutions (perhaps especially the criminal justice system), and even deny the existence of free will. Surely a world in which every aspect of human behaviour is hard-wired into our genes cannot comfortably exist with the concept of personal responsibility and free will to try (albeit not successfully for very long) to follow the moral law of right and wrong which people of faith believe has been written into our hearts by a loving and holy God.

*Collins, in **Peters**, 1997, Foreword*

Chapter summary

The question of free will

- It is commonly held that we need to be free to act to be responsible for actions.

- People have degrees of responsibility in different situations which mediate moral responsibility such as mitigating circumstances.

- External and internal factors limit freedom.

- Genetics and environment: we may be far less free than we think due to social upbringing and genetic predispositions.

- Self-restraint and willpower: some people seem to be able to resist temptation while others are tempted. B. F. Skinner argued that the idea of freedom was a mistake, and that humans are controlled by their environment.

- Within social settings individuals restrain themselves, giving up some individual freedoms for the benefits gained by living in a community.

- Societies have to work out ways of managing conflicts of interests.

Libertarianism

- Mill was concerned that the individual should not be crushed by the will of the mob (society) or the state (government).

- Mill felt that diversity and creativity added to the value of society and community as a whole.

- Libertarians hold that moral responsibility requires freedom – they believe that determinism is incompatible with freedom and moral responsibility.

- Conscience is an important religious idea which is linked to free moral action. In some religions it plays an important role as a tool for discerning what is right, or God's will, while other traditions have less of a place for it.

- Psychological accounts of conscience suggest it may in fact limit free action and control our actions.

- Choices are causally undetermined (we are not like balls on a snooker table).

- Individual conscience is very important – we should act with integrity.

Determinism

- Hard determinism is the view that we are not free and cannot be held morally responsible for our actions. All actions have a prior cause.

- Causes may be found in genetic predispositions and environmentally conditioned responses, external and internal, respectively. The misbehaviour gene, the Darrow case and the Milgram experiment all provide insights to this question.

- Soft determinism holds that some aspects of human beings are caused, but we are morally responsible for our actions because we can have influence over the causes.

- Soft determinists are criticised by hard determinists for failing to realise the extent to which human freedom is limited, and by libertarians for failing to realise the true extent of human freedom.

Religious perspectives on libertarianism and determinism

- The traditional Judeo-Christian view is that human beings are free, autonomous agents, responsible for their actions.

- An alternative view in Christian writings is that God has already decided who will be saved and who will not, predestination.

- Within Islam there is also a strong sense that what happens occurs because it is God's will that it should be – nothing can happen without it being in accordance with God's will, though people can still be free to act.

- Within Hinduism, Buddhism and Sikhism the role of causality has particular associations around the doctrine of karma. Human actions cause effects that are felt in the next life.

- Hard determinism challenges the possibility for the religious to lead the good life.

▓ Further reading and weblinks

Honderich, T. *How Free are You? The deterministic problem*, Oxford University Press, 2002. This is a lucid treatment of the arguments for free will and determinism and, coming from Honderich, it is very readable.

Mill, J. S. *On Liberty*, 1859. Available in many editions and on the internet at www.utilitarianism.com/ol/one.html. It is perhaps one of the most important texts of political philosophy in its valuation of the individual over the crowd. It can be seen as having links to many modern movements including the emancipation of women.

Mill, J. S. *The Subjection of Women*, 1869. Available online at http://ebooks.adelaide.edu.au/m/mill/john_stuart/m645s/.

Skinner, B. F. *Beyond Freedom and Dignity*, Penguin, 1971. Skinner's deterministic piece caused uproar and outcry among moral philosophers, but his behaviouristic psychology has gone on to influence education. Very cheap second-hand and very readable.

In this chapter you have:

- considered key elements of the debate about free will, especially how factors such as the environment and genetics might affect our freedom, how individual freedom is balanced by social contracts, how free wills may come into conflict

- considered important aspects of libertarianism including the nature of the moral self, human conscience and the causally undetermined choice

- considered important aspects of determinism including causality, both in hard and soft forms of determinism and the idea of internal and external causes
- examined religious perspectives of libertarianism and determinism and made some critical judgements about them
- considered both criticisms and strengths of libertarianism and determinism and made some judgement about the theory
- considered implications of libertarianism and determinism in a number of areas.

2 Virtue ethics

By the end of this chapter you will be able to:

- identify key distinguishing features of virtue theory

- describe the contribution of Aristotle to the virtues

- show an understanding of the modern contributors to virtue theory

- suggest what a virtue perspective of moral decision making adds to moral thinking

- suggest both criticisms and strengths of virtue theory.

Key philosophers

Aristotle (384–322 BCE)
Nicomachean Ethics

Elizabeth Anscombe (1919–2001)
Modern Moral Philosophy, 1958

Alasdair MacIntyre (1929–) *A Short History of Ethics*, 1966; *After Virtue, a Study in Moral Theory*, 1981

Philippa Foot (1920–) *Virtues and Vices*, 2002

Key questions

1 How can you be a better person?
2 What are the qualities of a good person?
3 Can practice make you a better person?

What is virtue theory?

Most moral theories try to work out what the right or good thing to do is. They tend to suggest a set of principles or rules that all human beings are bound by. According to utilitarians, the right thing to do is that which results in the greatest good for the greatest number. For situationists, it is the thing that causes the most loving consequence. In natural law, the right thing is that which is in accordance with the purpose of what it is to be human. Other moral theories suggest that there are no moral laws as such – morality is whatever is right for you, or that moral statements are simply emotive expressions (relativism and emotivism, respectively). Some moral theories understand good in terms of duties (for example Kant).

Virtue theory is different from these approaches. Instead of concentrating on what the right thing to do is, virtue theory is principally concerned with the idea of the human character and asks how you can be a better person. Most theories concentrate on defining principles by which we should act. Virtue theory is interested in defining good people and the qualities that make them good. Utilitarians and deontologists think that right behaviour comes before right character. Virtue theory puts this the other way round – right character comes before right behaviour. We should be less concerned with actions and consequences, and much more concerned with the character of the moral agent. The question 'What is it right or obligatory to do?' is not the only question. 'How should we be?' matters too, because it is only by becoming better people that we will do the right thing. In other words, while other ethical theories concentrate simply on the process of moral decision making, virtue theory is concerned about the process of how to become a moral person. Once you have become a moral person, you will do the right thing.

The roots of virtue theory are in Greek philosophy, especially Aristotle, and modern important contributors to virtue theory are Elizabeth Anscombe, Alasdair MacIntyre and Philippa Foot, though others have made valuable contributions.

Aristotle

Aristotle (384–322 BCE) was born at Stagirus, a Greek colony on the coast of Thrace. At the age of 17 he was sent to the intellectual capital of the Greek world, Athens, joined the Academy and studied under Plato. In later years, he gave his own lectures and set up his own school called the Lyceum.

In his work *Nicomachean Ethics*, Aristotle, writing in 350 BCE, argues that whenever we do something, we do it to gain an end, and that the ultimate end of all ends is the chief good, the greatest good.

Eudaimonia is the goal of life that everyone should pursue, and it is pursued for itself and not for some other good. It is not a means to an end but an end in itself and it is achieved through a life of virtuous action. In order to achieve that end we must practise, like archers who want to hit the target. By practising we improve our skills (virtue, or *arête* in Greek), and so become happy and live good lives. There are moral virtues that are qualities of character, such as courage, liberality, temperance and modesty, and we cultivate these by habit. There are 12 such moral virtues, but they fall between two vices – that of excess and that of deficiency. Courage is one of the virtues. If I do not have enough, then I am a coward. If I am excessively courageous, then I may become rash. Aristotle believed that all virtues lay at the mid-point between two vices, a **golden mean or virtuous mean**, as illustrated in the table below.

Although all of us could develop these virtues, only a few will do so. To cultivate them we must find the mean, controlling our emotions and behaviour towards others in different situations. We must behave in a proportionate way. We should not be excessively self-deprecating in the manner of Dickens' Uriah Heep in *David Copperfield* – we should be sincere. Our humour should not descend into buffoonery or extend to boorishness. If we are to be virtuous rather than simply emotive in our responses to people, self-control is essential. Aristotle believed that virtuous behaviour could become a habit, but at no time should we forget that we are behaving virtuously because it is right. By the same measure, we know how virtuous we are by how we spontaneously respond to situations. By seeing the virtues we do virtuous things.

Key terms

Eudaimonia: (as defined by Aristotle) what makes a person truly happy.

Golden mean or virtuous mean: the midway point between the vices of excess and deficiency.

Table 1 *Aristotle's view of virtuous mean*

Vice of deficiency	Virtuous mean	Vice of excess
Cowardice	Courage	Rashness
Insensibility	Temperance	Intemperance
Illiberality	Liberality	Prodigality
Pettiness	Munificence	Vulgarity
Humble-mindedness	High-mindedness	Vaingloriness
Want of ambition	Right ambition	Over-ambition
Spiritlessness	Good temper	Irascibility
Surliness	Friendliness/civility	Obsequiousness
Ironical deprecation	Sincerity	Boastfulness
Boorishness	Wittiness	Buffoonery
Shamelessness	Modesty	Bashfulness
Callousness	Just resentment	Spitefulness

Aristotle's view of people

Virtuous people enjoy doing good so face no moral dilemma.

Continent people do the virtuous thing most of the time but have to overcome moral dilemma.

Incontinent people face moral conflict but usually choose a vice.

Vicious people do not attempt to be virtuous.

Aristotle believed that every action is directed towards an aim. I get up in the morning because I want to go to work; I go to work because I want to earn a living and have a good career; I want earnings and career success so that I can live life well. There are superior and subordinate aims. Getting up in the morning is subordinate to earning a living. We do one thing to accomplish a greater thing. Ultimately, everything is subordinate to the supreme good, which is happiness. People have different ideas of happiness. Some seek pleasure, others seek honour (such as those who serve the community), and there are those who love contemplation (philosophers). It is the last of these that Aristotle believes to be the best.

''Tis but only a scratch!' When does courage turn to rashness?

Aristotle acknowledged that the virtues of one city may differ from those of another. He did not believe in an absolute platonic good beyond our world. He thought that good was found within this world. Different cities had different ideas of the ends to which they aimed, and the virtues that would take them towards those aims. The **supreme happiness** or eudaimonia that he talks about is one for the community, not just an individual. Virtues were understood by communities.

Four of the virtues later became known as cardinal virtues in Christian writing: prudence, justice, fortitude and temperance. They are related to one another and are needed for each other. I might know what is good, and what to do to make that goodness come about, but I may need to resist being tempted by other pleasures to see to that goodness. Another illustration of this is the phrase 'the road to hell is paved with good intentions'. I might show great courage in sacrificing myself, but in doing so I may go about things the wrong way. Later the term 'the seven cardinal vices' became popular in Christian writing, five of which were found in Aristotle's list.

Aristotle links ethical and intellectual excellence. He singles out five intellectual virtues which we need to act well and think correctly: prudence (or practical wisdom), intuitive intelligence, wisdom, scientific knowledge (which he called theoretical) and lastly craft or art (which he considers productive). He spends more time on prudence than any other. A prudent person deliberates well both about that which is good in specific areas, but also what it means to live well in general. Prudence gives insights into the truth about human action. There are additional intellectual virtues including deliberation, understanding, judgement and cleverness. Although these intellectual virtues may not be considered virtues today, they were judged important by Aristotle for working out what the golden mean was in a situation.

■ Key terms

Supreme happiness: the end to which virtue theory looks, an end which is both about an individual person's development and the whole community.

■ Take it further

Look up and read Aristotle's thinking about the virtues in his work *Nicomachean Ethics*.

■ Activities

1 Make a list of people whom you consider to be 'good people' in some sense and then try to identify what characteristics or virtues they exhibit which make them good.

2 Now compare your characteristics with those of others in your group. Have you identified common, discrete or contrasting 'virtues'?

3 Consider a familiar moral dilemma in terms of the character and virtues of the moral agent. How does this differ from thinking about the moral situation in terms of acts or consequences, for instance?

■ Modern virtue ethics

Elizabeth Anscombe

AQA Examiner's tip

Anscombe is not in the specification but is widely regarded as having triggered modern interest in virtue ethics.

Elizabeth Anscombe's paper 'Modern Moral Philosophy' (1958) initiated the modern revival of virtue theory. Her paper challenges both deontological and teleological ethical theories because both were preoccupied with a law conception of ethics which seemed to take no account of the emotions or moral psychology.

She was critical of moral theories which seemed to be prepared to allow any moral act of any kind if it brought about some good end. She argued that consequentialist thinking has come to dominate much of modern philosophy and it is wrong. Anscombe also thought that:

> the concepts of obligation, and duty – moral obligation and moral duty, that is to say – and of what is morally right and wrong, and of the moral sense of 'ought', ought to be jettisoned

*Reprinted in **Crisp and Slote**, 1997*

They are part of an idea of ethics that no longer survived, from a time when people still believed in a law giver such as God. Anscombe thought that thinking about ethics in terms of obligations to such rules was no longer necessary. She wrote:

> It would be a great improvement if, instead of 'morally wrong', one always named a genus such as 'untruthful', 'unchaste', 'unjust'. We should no longer ask whether doing something was 'wrong', passing directly from some description of an action to this notion; we should ask whether, e.g., it was unjust; and the answer would sometimes be clear at once.

*Reprinted in **Crisp and Slote**, 1997*

An idea of ethics defined as some universal legalistic principles needed to be changed. This was just as true for utilitarian ideas of the greatest good for the greatest number as it was for Kant's deontological categorical imperative.

Anscombe proposed a different way of studying ethics. We should think about the idea of a virtue and human flourishing, referring back to Plato and Aristotle. She also argued that some further development was necessary in coming to understand what we really mean by virtue.

Alasdair MacIntyre

In his book *After Virtue, a Study in Moral Theory* (1985), Alasdair MacIntyre thinks, like Anscombe, that modern morality has suffered a catastrophe. Modern ethics has lost sight of its roots. Modern philosophers have thrown the baby out with the bathwater. He writes 'we have – very largely, if not entirely – lost our comprehension, both theoretical and practical, of morality' (MacIntyre, 1981, p2). It is as if a global catastrophe has thrown us back into the Dark Ages. But instead of losing scientific knowledge, we have lost moral wisdom.

Like Anscombe, MacIntyre looks back to the writings of the ancient Greeks. The writings that told of great heroes such as Achilles and Odysseus show a vision of morality – you are what you do. The epic stories describe man in terms of his actions. His identity is defined by what he does. To judge a man is to judge his actions. The way in which

■ **Take it further**

Elizabeth Anscombe's paper 'Modern Moral Philosophy' which appeared in 1958 in the journal *Philosophy*, is available online (see the further reading and weblinks at the end of the chapter). Look it up on the internet and read it.

we behave provides an opportunity for others to judge our virtues and vices. It is in this society that the word virtue (*arête*), emerges.

In heroic society, courage is a measure of the quality of an individual and is essential to sustain a household and community. A courageous person is someone who can be relied on and so is important in friendship. Fidelity is also crucial for friendship, as it guarantees a person's will to support and help. A person who displays these virtues is a good person.

For MacIntyre then, moral questions should be explored in terms of how we should make the most of our human lives rather than simply whether we are following rules. James F. Keenan (1998) summarises virtue theory in three questions:

■ Who am I?
■ Who ought I to become?
■ How do I get there?

Virtues provide a way of estimating character, and suggest a direction in which you should go in order to become a better person. Virtue theory is person-centred and focused on our development. By practising actions that embody the virtue, we can grow in the virtues. Being virtuous requires practice, because we can be **excessive or deficient** in our behaviour. Our spontaneous behaviour illustrates the degree to which we are behaving in a virtuous manner. Self-knowledge is central – by knowing and understanding ourselves, we can practise to be better. Keenan likens this to good parenting. Good parenting is knowing how to help children to grow according to their own strengths and weaknesses.

Making good moral judgements

MacIntyre thinks that our ability to make good moral judgements comes from the development of good character. The virtues of life enable us to make good moral judgements. The judgements of virtuous people in working out what is good or evil are more important than moral laws. The virtuous person's judgement is a better guide to others than the rule of what is right or wrong and points to a better way of being than simply following the rules. The focus is not on the end of a given act, as with consequentialist thinking, but the complete end of a social practice and of a human life. It is in these terms that the morality of acts may be evaluated.

MacIntyre sees a moral society as one in which people recognise commonly agreed virtues and aspire to meet them. Those virtues improve and clarify themselves over time. MacIntyre looks back and identifies the virtues that have been picked up and passed on: from Aristotle, Christianity, democracy and so forth. MacIntyre thinks that virtues are understood from within a community of people who live in a certain way. Moral issues should be thought about in terms of the community practising the virtues, rather than in terms of following particular rules or seeking to bring about certain consequences. MacIntyre took this from the idea of the Christian community, a community developing and learning to follow in Jesus' footsteps. Other religions have perspectives of virtue such as those found in the Buddhist **Sangha**, the community of monks and nuns, lay and religious, who seek to live good or virtuous lives, and also in Sikhism where one endeavours to live a virtuous life. In both Buddhism and Sikhism, virtuous living brings good karma and so brings you a step closer to nirvana or God.

MacIntyre noted that there are differences between the virtues of the ancient Homeric world, which saw human excellence in terms of the

■ Key terms

Excessive or deficient: having too much or too little of a characteristic, e.g. rashness and cowardice for the virtue courage.

Sangha: the monastic community of ordained Buddhist monks or nuns.

■ Take it further

MacIntyre developed the notion of *internal* and *external* goods. An 'internal' good is integral to the activity or action occurring, and it is achieved through doing it. That is why it is called 'internal': it is 'inside' the activity. An 'external' good is something good or moral that comes out of doing the activity or action; it is called 'external' because it comes *out* of doing the activity.

warrior; Aristotle's idea of Athenian gentlemen; and the Christian virtues outlined by St Thomas Aquinas, who drew on Plato, Cicero, Ambrose, Gregory and Augustine to list four cardinal virtues – prudence, justice, temperance and fortitude/bravery – together with the theological virtues of faith, hope and charity (found in the New Testament in the Letters of Paul).

Prudence was central to both Aristotle and Aquinas. We must have both feet firmly on the ground so that we think practically and realistically. Our goals must be achievable and we should be moderate in reaching them. For MacIntyre, the virtues improve and clarify themselves over time. For the modern era Keenan suggests prudence, justice, fidelity, self-care and the distinctive Christian virtue of mercy. James Rachels suggests courage, honesty and loyalty to support friendship and stand up to the struggles of life.

For McIntyre, to understand how to achieve the good life, it is necessary to understand the different types of people in the modern world (rather than those of Aristotle's time): the manager, the aesthete and the therapist.

Activities

1. Compile a set of virtues suitable for the 21st century. Use the table on p27 and the paragraphs above to help you.

2. Decide on the 'vice of deficiency' and 'vice of excess' for each of your virtues.

3. In one paragraph for each, describe what you think a complete virtuous life and a completely virtuous society would look like.

4. Not long ago it was reported that a policeman had transformed his town, reducing antisocial behaviour by half. He set up a night school to teach children about medieval notions of respect and chivalry. More than a hundred children took the course which the policeman said instilled a sense of personal pride, of mannerly and compassionate behaviour and of respect for others.

   Devise a course for a 'virtue club'. What would the course do?

Philippa Foot

Philippa Foot is another very important figure in the modern virtue theory movement. She thinks that philosophers have neglected the subject of virtues and vices and is especially critical of meta ethical moral philosophers. She argues that virtues are beneficial in as much as human beings do not seem to get on well without them. In her book *Virtues and vices*, she writes:

> Nobody can get on well if he lacks courage, and does not have some measure of temperance and wisdom, while communities where justice and charity are lacking are apt to be wretched places to live, as Russia was under the Stalinist terror, or Sicily under the Mafia

Foot, 2002

Virtues are beneficial characteristics and things that a human being needs to have. Just as people need strength and health, so they need virtues; but whereas strength and health are excellences of the body, virtues are excellences of the will. It is by someone's moral intentions that they are judged. A scoundrel is still a scoundrel even if he is strong and healthy. Virtues also seem to relate to a person's innermost desires. Foot uses a passage from John Hersey's novel *A Single Pebble* to illustrate this:

> It was the head tracker's marvelous swift response that captures my admiration at first, his split second solicitousness when he heard a cry of pain, his finding in mid-air, as it were, the only way to save the injured boy. But there was more to it than that. His action, which could not have been mulled over in his mind, showed a deep, instinctive love of life, a compassion, an optimism, which made me feel very good.

Quoted by Foot, 2002

So virtues are both about our intentions and our wish to act. The virtues exist as a mean (or midway point) between two vices. It is possible to be tempted and for our virtues to become deficient or excessive. Virtues are a corrective against these temptations. We should have the virtue of hope because we are tempted by despair. We have the virtue of industriousness because idleness is a temptation. In some cases the virtues are there to prompt us to act when we might not otherwise, as is the case of justice and charity. It is easy for us to be attached to the good of ourselves and seek out our own interests, but it is more demanding to be attached to the good of others.

Foot also notes that in some moral situations being virtuous may be more demanding than in other situations. Consider these two examples. If I have an opportunity to steal and I am tempted to do so, this could shed light on a weakness in my lack of virtue, the more virtuous person being one who would not be tempted. On the other hand if I am impoverished with a starving family I may be sorely tempted to steal if the opportunity arises. In this case resisting the temptation says much more about the strength of my virtue than the first example because, in this situation, the need for the food is very much greater – the temptation much more powerful. These examples show how virtue theory looks far beyond the external outcomes or consequences of moral situations, and into the heart of the acting human being.

AQA Examiner's tip

Make sure you understand the differences between Anscombe and Foot, and particularly between MacIntyre and Aristotle. To enable kinaesthetic learning, write out the differences clearly and put them onto different-coloured sticky notes. Aristotle and MacIntyre highlighted that there are generally three types of people in society, but they each cited three *different* groups of people. Candidates often confuse which group belonged to which philosopher, and the way in which their lists of virtues differed.

Activities

1. Who do virtues benefit? Explain your answer.

2. Consider the school curriculum you are familiar with.
   a. Which subjects cultivate excellences of the body and which cultivate excellences of the will?
   b. What virtues does your school refer to in its publicity (prospectus, website, etc.) and how do these correspond to the curriculum?
   c. Should schools have more virtue learning?
   d. What might a virtue school look like?

3. Think of two more moral examples to illustrate how being virtuous may be more or less demanding depending on the situation.

4. Do you think that it is important for ethical theories to be sensitive to the challenge faced by people to be good? If so why/why not?

Allegory of Good Government

The virtues in practice: the Sala dei Nove

A powerful example of the virtues in operation can be seen from Ambrogio Lorenzetti's allegory of good and bad government, in the Sala dei Nove in the Palazzo Pubblico of Siena, painted between 1337 and 1339. The fresco was painted across all four walls of the hall of the Council of Nine, the city's administrators. The Nine were chosen every two months to ensure the good of the city. This example is important as, while it draws on the Christian idea of virtue, it is a secular expression of virtue. The city of Siena at this time was governed by secular authorities distinct from the Church, so it reflects an idea which might be relevant to secular ethical thinking in the modern world.

The Palazzo Pubblico in Siena is notable for its great *campo* (square) and tower which stands separate and equal to the dome and tower of Siena's Cathedral, an illustration of the separation of Church and Civic authority and the location of the centre of the city-state.

The fresco cycle covers three walls of the council chamber. The fourth wall has a window which lights the opposite wall on which is the Allegory of Good Government (see the image above). To one side of this are illustrated the effects of Good Government in town and countryside, and on the other is an illustration of Bad Government and its effects in the urban and rural contexts. The frescos are arranged to show the contrast between the happiness, wellbeing and order of life under good government and the darkness, chaos and suffering brought about by bad government. In the former, people are productive in business, there is dancing in the streets and a wedding. The different trades are able to go about their activity including a shoemaker, a teacher, a goldsmith and wine and meat sellers, and in the great city, building is under way. In the country the fields are cultivated, farmed and manicured with seeds being sown, vines growing, and peasants and travellers going about their business safely. The produce of the country is brought into the city illustrating that rural and urban life is in harmonious balance, and the figure of Security flies overhead. There is an openness about the city in terms of the diversity within and the accessibility to it from the country.

Allegory of Bad Government

On the opposite wall the effects of bad government are bleakly laid out. Discord and war are rife and there are examples of violence, murder, robbery and betrayal. The city has been heavily damaged, and beyond, in the country, the land is uncultivated, laid waste. Smoke rises from several places and the city seems turned in upon itself, cut off from the desolate countryside around it.

Both scenes have a corresponding government which is depicted through figures of the virtues and vices and some scenes of governance. In the Bad Government (see the image above), Tyranny presides. Above him fly Pride, Avarice and Vainglory; on either side sit Cruelty, Treason, Fraud, Furor, Division and War. Beneath, Justice is impotent, bound and defeated. The cords of the scales of Justice are broken. Above the country, the harp of fear flies. Around the fresco are various texts with sign messages for the images. 'Because each seeks only his own good in this city Justice is subjected to Tyranny', 'Where there is tyranny there is great fear', and 'There, where Justice is bound, no one is ever in accord for the Common Good, nor pulls the cord [i.e. of civic concord] straight [i.e. with force and full commitment]' (Starn, 1994, pp40–1). It is the duty of the citizen to keep citizens subject to Justice, to banish those who threaten it and to overthrow tyrants. Responsibility for the common good lies with every citizen, not merely the ruling order or class.

The sunlit end of the hall offers a different vision. The Court of the Good Government has two central figures. Highest seated to the right is the Common Good, with Faith, Charity and Hope flying above. Seated either side we see Peace, Fortitude, Prudence, Magnanimity, Temperance and Justice. To the left Justice is depicted again with Wisdom flying above. The virtue metes out Commutative and Distributive justice. Beneath sits Concord and to the right stand 24 Councillors holding the rope of concord. Texts beneath read, 'This holy Virtue [Justice], wherever she rules, induces to unity the many souls [of citizens], and they, gathered together for such a purpose, make the Common Good their Lord' (Starn, 1994, p53).

The virtues are virtues not just for those in government, but every citizen. Dire consequences follow if people's hearts are governed by vices rather than virtues.

The rule of Justice and the priority of the common good and the other virtues allow people of all trades and business to go about pursuing their separate interests. Good and bad government fundamentally and directly affect the quality of human lives. Whether we are well or badly governed makes a difference to our lives. We can choose whether our hearts and cities are governed by virtues or vices. The virtues and vices can be seen clearly from the effects and from the principles underpinning those effects. The fresco cycle is instructive for citizens and rulers to achieve well-being in life and it is an example of how virtue thinking was understood in Siena at that time.

Applying virtue theory

When thinking about the application of virtue theory one difficulty is that the theory is focused on far more than a particular moral situation, it is focused on the whole development of the person. It addresses the question of how people should learn to be moral. In other words, to apply virtue theory, you must look at the upbringing, education and general behaviour of people on a day-to-day basis. To simply look at a moral dilemma is to miss a crucial element of the work of the theory. Nevertheless, it is thought that good actions will come from the virtuous person: that charitable acts follow from charity, that prudent choices are made by the prudent.

When applying a theory to an issue, remember that your choice of issue is significant if you are going to evaluate the theory on the basis of how well it deals with your issue. Reread the section 'Tools for examining ethical theories' in the Introduction on pvi to remind yourself of some of the tools you have available.

Use the following checklist when applying virtue theory to an ethical issue. In the issue you are addressing, consider these questions:

1 Who are the moral agents (if there is more than one)?
2 In the moral options and choices available, what would be the virtuous thing to do (the brave thing, charitable thing, etc.)?
3 What sort of characteristics should they be demonstrating in this situation, for themselves and the sake of society?
4 Would certain options encourage bad or good habits if chosen?
5 Are there any conflicting virtues, i.e. does one option reflect one virtue while another option reflects another virtue?
6 To what extent are your conclusions dependent on agreement about what the virtues should be?
7 Are there competing virtues?
8 Do the conclusions you come to about what option to pursue seem reasonable or unreasonable?
9 Why is this?
   a Is it because of some other moral factor which virtue theory does not account for, and if so, which factor?
   b Is it because you value moral factors that differ from those expressed in the theory (such as the moral law, etc.)?
   c If so, can you justify why you value those factors over and above the ones which are important in the theory?
   d Is this a factor which is likely to be found in many ethical issues? In other words, does this flag up a more major problem with the theory as a whole, or just a problem with this particularly difficult issue?

Activity

Look through some recent news stories which reflect virtues or vices. Try to produce a picture of modern life in terms of the virtues and vices evident.

10 If the solution seems reasonable, how adequate do you think this moral example is in testing the theory? Might there be different kinds of examples which the theory has more trouble with?

■ Issues arising

Strengths and weaknesses of virtue ethics

Virtue theory encompasses all aspects of life rather than particular actions. It sees every moment as the possibility for acquiring or developing a virtue. Aquinas said that every human action is a moral action. What we do is what we are. Virtue theory is more proactive than dilemma-based ethics which responds to a difficult moral situation. It is involved in every aspect of human life. It has a different focus from that which interests teleological or deontological theorists (who are concerned with ends and acts, respectively).

Virtue theory provides an alternative route for drawing on the tradition of moral philosophy in a way that is different from the natural law approach. It avoids the pitfalls of ethical systems that espouse moral absolutes without indicating how people can learn to be moral in the way the absolutes suggest. It is an alternative ethical model that fits Christian ethics as it focuses on the kind of person we should be, something quite central to what it means to be a follower of Jesus, and what it means to be Christ-like. It also reaches beyond religious ethics as certain virtues can be seen as a civic expression of what would be good for society. Rather than simply looking for rules, it looks at the fundamental issue of what it means to be human. Virtue theory is concerned with the developing, growing inner human person and the character traits which make up that person.

However, there are a number of difficulties with virtue theory. Julia Annas (1992) thinks that ancient values may have something of value in them, but she also offers a warning:

> There is another attitude, equally harmful, I think, of romantic nostalgia: the feeling that it would be nicer if we could shed the problem-era that we have and go back to a very different set of problems, that ethics would be a kinder, gentler place if we could forget about hard cases and talk about friendship and the good life instead. Like much nostalgia, this is misplaced.
>
> *Annas, 1992*

An old idea is not necessarily a good idea. MacIntyre may be in danger of this misplaced nostalgia. Perhaps modern philosophers may have more to contribute to ethics than MacIntyre suggests because they are critical of past ethical systems.

In 'On some vices of virtue ethics' (1997), Robert Louden identifies other difficulties. Virtue theory does not provide answers to specific moral dilemmas such as euthanasia, nor does it provide a list of intolerable acts such as murder which we might want to condemn outright. Ethical theories are generally thought to provide such guidance but virtue theory does not quite do that. In addition, it is difficult to decide who is virtuous, as external acts that appear virtuous on the outside may have doubtful inner motives which cannot be perceived, and vice versa. The process of moral judgement is unclear in virtue theory.

Foot notes a further weakness. The virtues I have seem to benefit the people with whom I come into contact and in many cases me as well. So my wisdom benefits both myself and others with whom I have dealings. However, Foot notes that in matters of justice and charity, it may be that I must sacrifice my own interests for those of others. For instance I may have to make an unpopular call for justice for an individual who is disliked by many. I may have to give up luxuries so that the basic needs of others can be met. This aspect of virtue theory, the extent to which being moral is in my best interests, has troubled Foot over the years and she feels it is unresolved.

Is virtue ethics different from teleological and deontological ethics?

Virtue theory clearly has a different focus from teleological and deontological ethics. What virtue theory brings is a focus on human growth rather than a focus on the legislation and judiciary of morality, the focus on what is right and wrong.

It is concerned with how people can become moral, rather than simply what is moral and what is immoral. Rather than thinking of morality in terms of processes and consequences, systems and principles, it is focused on the character of the human being and has been very important in education. It considers the moral project as one which is about the development of human beings rather than simply the legislation or valuation of moral conduct. Other theories might judge actions or choices, but they do not offer suggestions about how people may become better at being good.

Perhaps virtue theory needs deontological ethics as well? In 'Are virtues no more than dispositions to obey moral rules?' Walter Schaller (1990) argues that moral virtues have only 'instrumental or derivative value'. Virtue theory relies on the concept of duty, our responsibility for acting in a certain way, and the idea that there are moral norms or absolutes. Arguably virtues supplement rather than replace deontological ethics.

Virtue ethics has a teleological dimension in that it is concerned with an idea of an end for human beings (the virtuous person) and an end for the human family or society (the virtues of the community).

Virtue ethics and a view of human nature

Virtue theory requires some sense of an idea about what human beings should be like, what they should be becoming, and from that idea the virtues are drawn. So we have suggestions that humans should be charitable and kind rather than selfish and greedy, for instance. The list of virtues and vices is based on an idea of human nature; a perspective of how human beings are which may be challenged by other ideas of human nature. Philippa Foot writes:

> It is possible ... that the theory of human nature lying behind the traditional list of virtues and vices puts too much emphasis on hedonistic and sensual impulses, and does not sufficiently take account of less straightforward inclinations such as the desire to be put upon and dissatisfied, or the unwillingness to accept good things as they come along.

Foot, 2002

Activities

1 Which is better – to be humble, or confident and assertive?

2 If you are going out clubbing is it more virtuous to be demure or brash and sexy?

3 Try to think of some virtues which clash? How do we decide which are good and which are not virtues at all?

If human nature is more diverse than Foot and other virtue theorists suggest then this poses a difficulty – are your virtues the same as my virtues? Just as MacIntyre tends to think in terms of the importance of community and tradition in agreeing on the virtues, in an increasingly diverse society with more attention being paid to different lifestyles and distinct personality types, it might be that a single list of virtues and vices is not suitable. Modern society is fragmented and diverse, with individuals living different lifestyles and flourishing, it would appear, in different ways. The kind of community in which people are united in a common project of character development envisaged by MacIntyre might be unrealistic in a modern diverse world.

Virtue ethics and religious approaches to morality

Virtue ethics is closely associated with religious traditions and a consideration of religious links might look to different religions. For instance, Aristotle's idea of virtue ethics was embraced within Christian thinkers such as Aquinas and has gone on to remain prominent in current Christian moral thinking. MacIntyre himself is a prominent Catholic philosopher. Christianity is concerned with human development, not simply moral acts.

Virtue ethics is also found in East Asian religious traditions. Hindu thinking is concerned with virtue or right conduct. In Buddhism compassion is the consummate Buddhist virtue. It shows both empathy with the suffering of others and a motivation to remove the suffering of others. The virtue of loving kindness is a concern for the well-being of others. Both Buddhism and Hinduism are concerned about the nature of the person, their motivations and intentions as much as their acts. Sikhism also is concerned with virtues. There are five virtues: *Sat* (truth), *Santokh* (contentment), *Daya* (compassion), *Nimrata* (humility) and *Pyare* (love). The ultimate goal of Sikhs is for their soul to merge with God, and to achieve this it is important to work hard at developing positive human qualities or virtues. Sikhs believe that they must develop their love of God by developing their compassion for God's creation.

Religions are concerned with human development and improvement and that involves developing certain characteristics. Because of this, virtue thinking is frequently an important part of religious moral development.

■ Extracts from key texts

Aristotle

Virtue, then, being of two kinds, intellectual and moral, intellectual virtue in the main owes both its birth and its growth to teaching (for which reason it requires experience and time), while moral virtue comes about as a result of habit, whence also its name (ethike) is one that is formed by a slight variation from the word ethos (habit). From this it is also plain that none of the moral virtues arises in us by nature; for nothing that exists by nature can form a habit contrary to its nature. For instance the stone which by nature moves downwards cannot be habituated to move upwards, not even if one tries to train it by throwing it up ten thousand times; nor can fire be habituated to move downwards, nor can anything else that by nature behaves in one way be trained to behave in another. Neither by nature, then, nor contrary to nature do the virtues arise in us; rather we are adapted by nature to receive them, and are made perfect by habit.

Again, of all the things that come to us by nature we first acquire the potentiality and later exhibit the activity ... but the virtues we get by first exercising them, as also happens in the case of the arts as well. For the things we have to learn before we can do them, we learn by doing them, e.g. men become builders by building and lyre-players by playing the lyre; so too we become just by doing just acts, temperate by doing temperate acts, brave by doing brave acts ...

Again, it is from the same causes and by the same means that every virtue is both produced and destroyed, and similarly every art; for it is from playing the lyre that both good and bad lyre-players are produced. And the corresponding statement is true of builders and of all the rest; men will be good or bad builders as a result of building well or badly. For if this were not so, there would have been no need of a teacher, but all men would have been born good or bad at their craft.

This, then, is the case with the virtues also; by doing the acts that we do in our transactions with other men we become just or unjust, and by doing the acts that we do in the presence of danger, and being habituated to feel fear or confidence, we become brave or cowardly.

The same is true of appetites and feelings of anger; some men become temperate and good-tempered, others self-indulgent and irascible, by behaving in one way or the other in the appropriate circumstances. Thus, in one word, states of character arise out of like activities. This is why the activities we exhibit must be of a certain kind; it is because the states of character correspond to the differences between these. It makes no small difference, then, whether we form habits of one kind or of another from our very youth; it makes a very great difference, or rather all the difference.

Aristotle, 350 BCE

Alasdair MacIntyre

The nature of virtues

A virtue is an acquired human quality the possession and exercise of which tends to enable us to achieve those goods which are internal to practices and the lack of which effectively prevents us from achieving any such goods. Later this definition will need amplification and amendment. But as a first approximation to an adequate definition it already illuminates the place of the virtues in human life. For it is not difficult to show for a whole range of key virtues that without them the goods internal to practices are barred to us, but not just barred to us generally, barred in a very particular way.

It belongs to the concept of a practice as I have outlined it – and as we are all familiar with it already in our actual lives, whether we are painters or physicists or quarterbacks or indeed just lovers of good painting or first-rate experiments or a well thrown pass – that its goods can only be achieved by subordinating ourselves within the practice in our relationship to other practitioners. We have to learn to recognize what is due to whom; we have to be prepared to take whatever self-endangering risks are demanded along the way; and we have to listen carefully to what we are told about our own inadequacies and to reply with the same carefulness for the facts.

> In other words we have to accept as necessary components of any
> practise with internal goods and standards of excellence the virtues
> of justice, courage, and honesty.

MacIntyre, 1985

■ Chapter summary

What is virtue theory?

- Virtue theory asks how you can be a better person – it defines good
  people and the qualities that make them good.

- To judge a man is to judge his actions. The way in which we behave
  provides an opportunity for others to judge our virtues and vices.

Aristotle

- Aristotle argued that whenever we did something, we did it to gain
  an end, and that the ultimate end of all ends was the chief good, the
  greatest good.

- To achieve that end we must practise, like archers who want to hit the
  target. By practising, we improve our skills (virtue/*arête*) develop good
  habits and so become happy and live good lives.

- Human characteristics can be excessively developed or may be lacking
  in development. Aristotle argued that the golden mean was the
  right virtuous point of development for human characteristic and he
  suggested a number of virtues themselves.

Modern virtue ethics

Elizabeth Anscombe

- Anscombe triggered the modern discussion about virtue ethics. She
  was critical of modern moral thinking and felt modern society was
  dislocated from the old traditions.

- She felt that any ethical system simply defined in terms of universal
  legalistic principles was problematic.

Alasdair MacIntyre

- Modern morality has suffered a catastrophe – wisdom is lost, and only
  fragments of the ancient traditions remain.

- In heroic societies virtues had meaning and a person who displayed
  virtues was a good person.

- Keenan summarises virtue theory in the questions: Who am I? Who
  ought I to become? How do I get there?

- Virtue theory is person-centred and focused on our development. By
  practising actions that embody the virtue, we can grow in the virtues.

- Our ability to make good moral judgements comes from the
  development of good character.

- The focus is not on the end of a given act but the complete end of a
  social practice and a human life.

- MacIntyre sees a moral society as one in which people recognise
  commonly agreed virtues and aspire to meet them. Those virtues
  improve and clarify themselves over time.

Philippa Foot

- Foot argues that virtues are beneficial and necessary as human beings do not get on well without them.

- Virtues also seem to relate to a person's innermost desires, they are about our intentions and our wish to act.

- In some moral situations being virtuous may be more demanding than in other situations.

Example of virtue theory in practice

- Ambrogio Lorenzetti's allegory of good and bad government serves as an illustration of how the virtues or vices of the people and government are reflected in the town and country.

- Virtues in government and people lead to a happy flourishing city while vices lead to war, famine and fear.

Evaluating virtue ethics

- Virtue theory is person-centred and focused on our development.

- Virtues provide a way of estimating character, and suggest a direction in which you should go in order to become a better person.

- Virtue theory encompasses all aspects of life rather than particular actions.

- Rather than simply looking for rules, virtue theory looks at the fundamental issue of what it means to be human.

- Arguably, virtue theory ultimately depends on moral duty and moral absolutes.

- Virtue theory is interested in the ultimate ends of human society and the human person in that society.

- Virtue theory depends on some idea about what human beings should be like to draw virtue from. Different ideas about human nature lead to different virtues. How useful is virtue theory in a pluralistic and diverse society?

- Virtue ethics is closely associated with religions as they are frequently concerned with human development.

Further reading and weblinks

Anscombe, G. E. M. *Modern Moral Philosophy*, 1958. Originally published in *Philosophy* 33, No. 124 (January 1958), but available online at www.philosophy.uncc.edu/mleldrid/cmt/mmp.html. Its availability on the internet makes it accessible, though it requires concentration and a good dictionary of philosophy to hand. Anscombe initiated the modern discussion.

Crisp, R. and Slote, M. *Virtue Ethics (Oxford Readings in Philosophy)*, Oxford University Press, 1997. A fantastic collection of essays by all of the key thinkers, Anscombe, Murdoch, MacIntyre, Foot and Hursthouse among others.

Foot, P. *Virtues and Vices and Other Essays in Moral Philosophy*, Clarendon Press, 2002. The book has much more to offer than a reflection on virtues (not least for this course chapters on free will and determinism).

MacIntyre, A. *After Virtue: A study in moral theory*, 3rd edn, University of Notre Dame Press, 2007. The original 1981 version was published by Duckworth. MacIntyre was not the first modern philosopher to engage in virtue theory, but his work has spawned nearly three decades of philosophical and political discussion and has directly informed political debates and trends in both the USA and the UK.

In this chapter you have:

- explored the key features of virtue theory and how it is distinguished from deontological and teleological theories
- investigated the contribution of Aristotle to the virtues, especially in terms of the aims of human life, the golden mean and supreme happiness
- considered the modern discussion of virtue theory, the notable contributions of Anscombe, Foot and MacIntyre
- considered what a virtue perspective of moral decision making adds to moral thinking
- considered both criticisms and strengths of virtue theory.

3 Religious views on sexual behaviour and human relationships

By the end of this chapter you will be able to:

- identify and describe different religious and philosophical approaches to issues of sexuality and relationships

- explain the role of sacred texts, institutions and also individual responses in religious approaches to issues of sexuality and relationships

- consider strengths and weaknesses of libertarian, feminist and religious approaches to issues of sexuality and relationships.

Link

For more on agape love see p38 of *AQA Religious Studies: Ethics AS*.

Key questions

1 Should religion have anything to do with sexual behaviour?

2 Is religion too patriarchal to be the basis of a sexual ethic in the modern world?

3 Should sexual ethics be based on what the majority of people in society think to be true?

4 Are religious views of sexuality and marriage hampered by backward ideas of what is natural or fixed ideas of the roles of men and women?

Religion and love

Love is an important idea in many religions. In Christianity love is thought of in different ways. Perhaps the highest of all kinds of love is agape love, unconditional love which expects nothing in return. This is the kind of love which inspires people to help a stranger. This kind of love is sometimes self-sacrificing, and is always thoughtful and volitional. In other words, it is an active love, a willed love, rather than something you fall into. In Buddhism this is known as *Advesa* and *maitri*. Unconditional love exemplifies the detached compassion necessary for enlightenment. In the Mahayana Buddhist tradition the self-sacrificial nature of this kind of love motivates Bodhisattvas to delay the final step to nirvana in order that others may be helped.

In the ancient world, *eros* is erotic, sexual love. It is often associated with love at first sight, the passions of love, the love that seeks for wholeness, or togetherness, ultimately expressed in lovemaking. It is not necessarily virtuous and can lead the moral person astray. At times erotic love has been considered to represent a very dangerous focus on the physical body, while missing the virtuous intellectual love or unconditional love. Ascetic religious traditions are suspicious of such an emphasis on the physical satisfaction offered by giving oneself to sensual pleasures. However, other religious traditions see an important role in sensual erotic love, in the natural intimacy of a physical relationship. In Buddhism, sensual or sexual love can be an obstacle to enlightenment as it encourages attachment. In Hinduism this kind of love is *kāma*.

Philial love is brotherhood or sisterhood. This is often thought of in terms of friendship, kin of the same kind, religious, ethnic or cultural. This love is found in the bonds of people united in a community group. This can be a profoundly moral form of love, in that it characterises natural bonds that exist in groups, but there are also dangers within it. In encouraging clan identity and group honour it can lead to inter-group tensions and conflict. It is a love which prefers those like me over those unlike me, so it is not inclusive as agape love is. Philial love assumes a mutuality, a reciprocity from others of the same group.

Love is also thought of in terms of compassion, caring or kindness, the kind of empathetic sensitivity which looks out for and looks after someone. There is a tenderness in compassion, which is illustrated in the way a parent looks after a child – intimately and sensitively.

For some this extends to others, even strangers, and is characterised by a thoughtfulness that sees when another is in need. In Hinduism compassionate love is *karuna* while *prem* is holy love.

Divine love is a feature of many religions. In Christianity, God is described as being love. In Islam, Sufis focus on divine love, a holy beauty. In Judaism, God commands that his people love Him and their neighbours (Deuteronomy 6:5).

The ethics of sex and relationships

Sex and relationship ethics encompasses a wide variety of issues related to marriage and sex, gender, gender orientation and attitudes and values related to reproduction, sexual pleasure and commitment. There is a great deal of disagreement about these issues today. Religion is sometimes viewed in the secular world as having outdated views of marriage which reflect patriarchal cultures and biological ignorance. So, for instance, women are seen in misguided and utilitarian terms solely as mothers, with an ability to reproduce, though women are not able to do so for half of their lives. Religons have rarely given women equal status to men in relationships and in marriage. Some say the secular world is just as guilty through the objectification of women for sexual pleasure, and what is needed is cultural change both within religion and outside religion. Some argue that patriarchal cultural attitudes have distorted authentic religious teaching.

Exploring religious attitudes to sex and relationships is difficult. There are diverse and contradictory perspectives within most religious traditions, and these perspectives are frequently based on quite different interpretations of the religious tradition itself both in terms of how sacred texts are interpreted and how they are used. Within every tradition explored in this book there are lively discussions about what the religion is saying, or should be saying. The starting points for this chapter are contested by scholars and religious authorities.

Ancient and modern attitudes to sex and marriage

The ancient world had competing views of sex. The ancient Greek philosopher Pythagoras believed that humans should abstain from the physical, and live a quiet contemplative life. Pythagoreans believed that their souls were imprisoned in the body and that they had to free them to move to a new life form. The physical obstructs the soul's progress. Because sex inhibits this progress, it is not holy. This division of the world between the physical and the spiritual is called **dualism**. The ancient Greek **Stoics** took a similar line and regarded with disapproval the sense of loss of control and animal instinct involved in sexual excitement and orgasm.

The Cyrenaics, established by Aristippus in the 5th century BCE, were a group who celebrated physical pleasure and led a life of sensual enjoyment. They saw immediate physical pleasures as the supreme good and pursued them.

The ancient Israelites also had a more positive attitude to sex and reproduction. This is seen in the *Song of Songs*, in which a couple express the sensual erotic beauty that they see in each other. There were also certain rules that recognised the importance of sex in marriage. Newly married men were excused from military service for one year to allow the couple to enjoy each other.

Key terms

Dualism: the division of the world between the physical and the spiritual.

Stoics: a group of Greek philosophers who regarded with disapproval the sense of loss of control and animal instinct involved in sexual excitement.

In the modern world attitudes to sex and relationships are changing. Sexual pleasure is often presented as a holy grail, pursued purely for its immediate physical satisfaction. This egoistical attitude observes that, with mutual consent, any form of sex is morally right. Monogamy and commitment beyond the moment are not required. Sex is an activity negotiated between the relevant parties and, as such, it falls outside religious teachings or absolute moral laws and marriage is not a prerequisite. The freedom of the individual is paramount.

The paradox in contemporary western culture is apparent in the rising concern over sexual crimes, rising teenage pregnancy rates and the proliferation of sexually transmitted diseases, most notably HIV and AIDS. We seem to have greater difficulty in maintaining committed loving relationships and the rate of divorce is increasing. The values underpinning relationships seem to have changed. People differ in their views over the nature of sex education in schools and when it should be taught, as well as the availability and nature of pornography. Some see this as a decay in traditional values, as undermining the family and creating a social disaster, with more abortions than ever before and more children living in poverty as a result of marital breakdown. Others see those values as restrictive, preventing the realisation of their true sexual identity.

Marriage in transition

In his book *Living Together and Christian Ethics* (2002), Adrian Thatcher summarises some research on marriage in the modern world:

1 In the UK, more people enter marriage from cohabitation than from a single state.

2 Cohabiters are just as likely to return to the single state as to enter marriage.

3 The connection between marriage and parenthood has been weakened. This follows an earlier separation of sex and marriage which took place in the 1960s.

4 Some people choose cohabitation as an alternative to marriage rather than simply as a preparation for it. Some have seen cohabitation as a version of a trial marriage, but others suggest it is a looser, less committed kind of marriage. Marriage is declining in importance.

Roger Crook, in his book *An introduction to Christian ethics*, argues that the picture of family life is often sentimentalised and idealised and the idea of a typical marriage, out of love, and a typical family life (her indoors, him the breadwinner) is simplistic (Crook, 2002, p116). There were always complex situations, people marrying for all sorts of reasons, in loving and less loving relationships. However, the changing patterns in society in the last century have affected these issues and Crook identifies three major forces of change:

1 The changing status of women is a major factor. Women have moved into the workplace and make up over 50 per cent of the workforce. Growing financial independence and a change in roles in terms of provision for childcare has led to a reconsideration of men's and women's roles.

2 The development of safe methods of contraception and availability of abortion has meant pre-marital sexual relationships do not carry the same risks as they did a century ago (though there are of course new risks in the spread of STDs).

3 We have a deepening understanding of sexuality across a number of different fields. In biological terms we now have a better

What role does marriage have in the modern world?

understanding of human sex drives outside any concept of love. In social terms we now understand that sexuality affects how people interact with each other generally, not simply in terms of sex itself. We also have a much better understanding of our romantic notion of love and how it tends to generate an idealised perception of the other person.

Gareth Moore (1998) notes that in the past religious authorities saw many elements of sexual ethics as being taken for granted and the focus was on the purpose of sex, what kinds of sexual acts were permitted and in what situations. The purpose of sex was for bringing children into the world, so it was very much about reproduction. Children need a loving family so marriage was necessary. As a result, sex before marriage and adultery were wrong. Sexual activity not about reproduction was wrong. He writes:

> Masturbation, contraception, bestiality and anal and oral sex were all in a deep sense contrary to the will of God.
>
> *Moore, 1998*

But now things have changed, not just in Christian ethics but in all religious ethics:

> Today, the old certainties are disappearing, and sex and its place in human relationships is one of the most controversial areas of modern Christian ethics.
>
> *Moore, 1998*

In the west there is a wide sense of discontentment with traditional religious sexual ethics.

■ Jewish and Christian approaches to sex and relationships

Sacred scripture

The Hebrew Scriptures depict sex and sexuality in many different ways. The stories within contain examples of rape and adultery, and elsewhere express profound values of commitment in love. On the one hand the textual sources represent sex as relational, **unitative** and sensual, while on the other there are tensions between sex and holiness.

Sex as relational, unitative and sensual

In his study of Christian ethics, Roger Crook (2001, p120) argues that the Bible itself sees sex as a normal part of life. Sex and human sexual nature is God given, part of God's creation, and through sex humanity is fulfilled through the unity of man and woman coming together (Genesis 2:24). Unity in the biblical sense is male and female together – heterosexuality is presented as the norm. Sexuality is part of human nature, a characteristic of all human beings. The Bible presents sex as good in as much as it is an important part of God's purpose in creating man and woman. The Bible presents sex in terms of a relationship and the phrase 'to know' is used to mean this. Knowing means being involved deeply with another person in a close and intimate relationship or communion.

In Genesis the purpose of human difference, in the male and female forms of humanity, is in part seen as the coming together of that difference in the sexual union of man and woman (Genesis 2:24–25). A vivid representation of the sensuality of that union is found in the *Song of Songs* (or *Song of Solomon*). A poetic vision of the sensual love between a bride and bridegroom could be described as a celebration of being in love, with all the erotic physical passions that accompany that sensation. Many authors writing about biblical sexual ethics refer to the *Song of Songs*, perhaps in an attempt to correct an image that religious ethics are in some way de-sexual – that holiness is the opposite of sensuality. This extract reflects this passion.

The bride singing to the bridegroom:

> All night long on my bed I looked for the one my heart loves; I looked for him but did not find him. I will get up now and go about the city, through its streets and squares; I will search for the one my heart loves. So I looked for him but did not find him. The watchmen found me as they made their rounds in the city. Have you seen the one my heart loves? Scarcely had I passed them when I found the one my heart loves. I held him and would not let him go till I had brought him to my mother's house, to the room of the one who conceived me.

> **New International Bible**, *Song of Solomon, 3:1–10*

The bridegroom singing to the bride:

> Behold, you are beautiful, my love, behold, you are beautiful! Your eyes are doves behind your veil. Your hair is like a flock of goats, moving down the slopes of Gilead. Your teeth are like a flock of shorn ewes that have come up from the washing, all of which bear twins, and not one among them is bereaved. Your lips are like a scarlet thread, and your mouth is lovely. Your cheeks are like halves of a pomegranate behind your veil. Your neck is like the tower of David, built for an arsenal, whereon hang a thousand bucklers, all of them shields of warriors. Your two breasts are like two fawns, twins of a gazelle, that feed among the lilies. Until the day breathes and the shadows flee, I will hie me to the mountain of myrrh and the hill of frankincense. You are all fair, my love; there is no flaw in you. Come with me from Lebanon, my bride; come with me from Lebanon.

> **New International Bible**, *Song of Solomon, 3:1–4, 4:1–7*

Sara Sviri (1995) writes that:

> As we listen to these evocative, ancient verses we too may become emotionally involved, touched by the direct and unabashed passion which speaks with such strong erotic images.

> It speaks in a language which is extremely sensual about familiar areas hidden within our own selves.

> It expresses the well-known inner emotional drama, as well as the outer frustrations and gratification …

> Its universal erotic sets of metaphors may stir within us dormant emotions and sensations.

> *Sviri, 1995*

Sexuality and holiness

At the same time there is a separation of sexuality and the sacred in the Bible. Tikva Frymer-Kensky (1995) writes that this can be seen in Moses' commandment to Israel to abstain from sex for three days before the revelation from God at Mt Sinai (Exodus 19:15). There are other examples of such a separation in 1 Samuel 21:4–5, and notable in the separation between priests' functions and sexuality, with very high expectations of priests regarding their sexual conduct and also the family of priests (1 Samuel 2.22–25).

As with the Stoics and Pythagoreans, early Christians raised the status of celibacy to one that was more holy. Jesus did not marry, although he did have a positive view of marriage. The first recorded miracle by Jesus was at the wedding of Cana and he repeated the teachings of the Hebrew Scriptures on the importance of marriage and had a stricter interpretation of divorce.

St Paul is noted for his negative view of sex, recommending celibacy in 1 Corinthians 7:25–40 in the light of the imminent end of the world. However, he acknowledges that celibacy is a special gift that is not for all, and he warns that it is better to be married than to commit sin and risk damnation. St Paul does have other things to say about sex and marriage. In his letter to the Corinthians he stresses the sense of deep mutuality that exists in a couple's relationship. He writes:

> Each man should have his own wife and each woman her own husband. The husband should fulfil his marital duty to his wife, and likewise the wife to her husband. The wife's body does not belong to her alone but to her husband. In the same way, the husband's body does not belong to him alone but also to his wife.

New International Bible, *1 Corinthians 7:2–4*

This principle is a powerful statement: any sexual activity with someone other than the spouse means the giving away of that which we do not have to give away. I must not offer my body to anyone other than my wife because it is hers. The New Testament then is quite strict on the view that couples come together in unions of one plus one. Other forms of marriage that include more than one partner, such as polygamy, are against Christian teaching, as is adultery. St Paul also offers a theological understanding of marriage, as reflecting Christ's relationship with the Church (see Ephesians Chapter 5). Marriage is compared to the Trinity, as the two become one in a relationship.

It is important to note that Jesus' attitude to sinners reflects a forgiving and open approach to people who have a complex sexual history. The Samaritan woman at the well is described as someone who has had many husbands and yet this conversation, the longest dialogue in the New Testament, is not filled with a moral diatribe against her for her conduct, but a deep and open conversation in which Jesus tells her about the water of eternal life and she asks how she may get such water. It is the start of her journey into faith. She is a Samaritan woman of doubtful virtue, but this does not matter to Jesus. In fact he breaks many taboos of the time in even talking to her. Crook describes this in terms of actions being immoral, rather than people being immoral.

The Christian Church, sex and relationships

Sex, the body and sin

Christian attitudes to sex and marriage are influenced by the ancient cultures into and out of which the religion was born. Christian writers sometimes portrayed sex in a negative light – as with St Augustine who considered sex to be a sin except for the purpose of reproduction. Aquinas

Activity

Try to identify from this review of sacred texts in Judaism and Christianity conflicting attitudes towards sex and relationships.

held a more positive view of the enjoyment of sex, although he still retained the idea that sex had to be connected to reproduction.

Almost all Christian monastic communities have been celibate and the Roman Catholic Church still advocates celibacy for its priests, while Protestant denominations do not. Martin Luther left his monastery and married, while Erasmus praised marriage as the natural state and thought of celibacy as an unnatural state. He argued that marital sexuality was in part for the purpose of pleasure rather than reproduction alone.

Today, marriage is seen as the norm for lay people. Most Churches hold that sex outside marriage, adultery, masturbation and homosexual sex are all sinful. They come to those conclusions either from a scriptural standpoint – New Testament statements about marriage or sex forming the basis of moral judgements – or from a natural law standpoint, which uses Aquinas's theory to make judgements about the purpose of human beings, and from that to determine which sexual activities fit such a purpose and which do not.

The older idea that sex and the body were sinful has been replaced by a more complex way of thinking about it. For instance, in the Roman Catholic Church the dignity and worth of the body is declared:

> Though made of body and soul, man is one. Through his bodily composition he gathers to himself the elements of the material world. Thus they reach their crown through him, and through him raise their voice in free praise of the Creator. For this reason man is not allowed to despise his bodily life.

Gaudium et spes, 1996, Chapter 14

Ideas that the function of sex was inherently sinful or that human sexuality is in some way dirty are put to one side in some modern Christian teachings on marriage.

The purpose of marriage

Sexual relationships are understood to be the preserve of marriage, a faithful, exclusive and ordinarily lifelong union. Men and women are equal, but created different, and united physically in lovemaking. It is a sacred union, part of God's divine plan. Sexual pleasure is a gift from God, and child rearing is part of the purpose of marriage. Marriage is understood in theological terms. Adrian Thatcher (2002) writes that Catholic and Eastern Orthodox Christianity understands marriage in terms of a **sacrament**. A marriage between baptised Christians is a shared commitment to Jesus Christ, a realisation of Christian identity, or the pursuit of holiness and sanctity. It is an ascetic practice in that it requires renunciation of others and includes the giving and receiving of gifts, so it is like the Trinitarian way in which God is love.

> **Key terms**
>
> **Sacrament:** traditionally, an outward sign of inward grace ordained by God.

The Christian Church saw the purpose of marriage as fidelity (*fides*) to one another, procreation (*proles*) and union of the parties (*sacramentum*). Marriage is a sacred event, not simply a legal arrangement. Christian ethics have focused on the purpose of sex as the key feature for making judgements on particular actions. There were two ways of establishing the purpose. One was to use sacred Scripture, and the other natural law. The Bible was interpreted as suggesting that sex was for having children – in Genesis, the Lord sent man forth to multiply, and that matched the view ascribed to by natural law. The proponents of natural law (most clearly expounded by Thomas Aquinas) believed that by identifying what the function of the human being was, they could see what should and should not be done. Sex led to reproduction, and so that was the purpose of the sexual organs. They should not be used for anything other than reproduction, and contraception was forbidden as preventing God's purpose. Sexual activities that did not lead to the birth of children (including masturbation, anal sex and oral sex) were also forbidden. Today, the use of artificial contraception is prohibited by the Roman Catholic Church as it prevents God's purpose from taking place. As children require a stable environment, marriage is necessary. Extra-marital and pre-marital sex undermine the family and risk bringing children into an insecure environment.

More recently, greater emphasis has been placed on the unitive element. Until the 20th century there was no link between sex and love in Christian theology. During the 20th century, the Churches moved to develop an understanding of sex that is rooted in love. A number of documents illustrate the recognition of sex as a uniting, bonding, healing and affirming feature between a married couple. In its document *Marriage and the Church's Task* (1978), the Church of England notes that:

> The commitment is made in love for love ... It is a profound sharing of present experience. As such, it also anticipates the sharing of future experience. It is a commitment through time. It embraces the future as well as the present. It intends and promises permanence ... The polyphony of love finds expression in the lovers' bodily union. This is not to be comprehended simply in terms of the two individuals' experiences of ecstatic pleasure. Such it certainly may be; but it is always more. It is an act of personal commitment which spans past, present and future. It is celebration, healing, renewal, pledge and future. Above all it communicates the affirmation of mutual belonging ... [Marriage] is a relational bond of personal love, a compound of commitment, experience and response, in which the commitment clothes itself in the flesh and blood of a living union.

Church of England, 1978, pp87–9 and 99

Similarly, the Roman Catholic Church has stated:

> This love is uniquely expressed and perfected through the marital act. The actions within marriage by which the couple are united ultimately and chastely are noble and worthy ones ... these actions signify and promote the mutual self-giving by which spouses enrich each other with a joyful and thankful will.

Pastoral Constitution, Part 2, Chapter 1

Formally, Catholic Christianity maintains that the life-giving dimension of each act of sex is a primary function and, within the same documents as those quoted above, the Roman Catholic Church restates the traditional view: 'the true practice of **conjugal** love, and the whole meaning of family life which results from it, have this aim; that the couple be ready with stout hearts to cooperate with the love of the Creator and the Saviour, who through them will enlarge and enrich his own family day by day' (*Pastoral Constitution*, Part 2, Chapter 1).

Complementary and egalitarian views of Christian marriage

Some Christians understand marriage in terms of complementarity. Men and women offer complementary and distinct gifts and roles. Men have a greater responsibility than women. They have headship of the couple and family and must protect and provide for the family.

Key terms

Conjugal: married lovemaking.

The husband and wife are of equal worth before God, since both are created in God's image. The marriage relationship models the way God relates to his people. A husband is to love his wife as Christ loved the church. He has the God-given responsibility to provide for, to protect, and to lead his family. A wife is to submit herself graciously to the servant leadership of her husband even as the church willingly submits to the headship of Christ. She, being in the image of God as is her husband and thus equal to him, has the God-given responsibility to respect her husband and to serve as his helper in managing the household and nurturing the next generation.

Southern Baptist Convention, 2000, Article XVIII

Other Christians take a more egalitarian view that men and women are equal before God. Matthew 20:25–26a, Mark 10:42 and Luke 22:25 lead some to conclude that Jesus forbids any hierarchy of relationships:

But Jesus called the disciples and said, 'You know that the rulers of the gentiles lord it over them and their superiors act like tyrants over them. That's not the way it should be among you'.

New International Bible, *Matthew 20: 25–26a*

Maria-Teresa Porcile-Santisco writes that the basic principles which underpin Christian thinking on sexuality are as follows:

The principle of equality: Men and women have the same nature with a divine origin and relationship ... The principle of sexual differentiation. The two sexes are not different in value but in function, and maleness and femaleness are not superior or inferior to the other, but simply different from each other. The principle of the drive to union, the principle of integration. Just as the sexes are equal and different, they tend to union. The principle of sublimation (occasional, or permanent in the case of celibacy). The final principle concerning sexuality is the possibility of surmounting it through sublimation.

Porcile-Santisco, 1991

Porcile-Santisco's argument is that the Church has always promoted equality between men and women.

Rosemary Radford Ruether (1991) argues that there are many traditions within Christianity and some of them were ambivalent or less than supportive about the idea of women's equivalent dignity or status. She notes that St Augustine denied that women possessed the image of God within them, conferring that on men only. Augustine stated that men have headship, meaning superiority, over women. Reuther argues that this leads to the current Roman Catholic teaching that only men can be priests. Controversy remains about the traditions within Christianity and their ethical implications for understanding current perspectives of sex and marriage.

Homosexuality

In western society – and in the UK in particular – there is a growing assumption that there is no moral issue about same-sex relationships beyond the issues that apply to heterosexual relationships. There is a growing belief that homosexuality is not about choosing what sexual acts to perform, but a disposition of attraction to members of the same sex, which is possibly biological or genetic in origin. Nevertheless, there is

Activities

1 How could you argue that contemporary Christian attitudes to sexuality and relationships have a lot to offer modern society?

2 How could you argue that Christian attitudes to sexuality and relationships are challenged by the values of the modern world, and which values in particular?

still a stigma attached to homosexuality in some societies and cultures and there are strongly held views that it is immoral. The common derogatory use of the word 'gay' in British society is one example of this, while a more extreme manifestation is the nail-bombing of a gay bar in London's Soho district in 1999. In the early part of the 20th century, homosexual acts were crimes, and homosexuality was considered a mental illness for which appalling treatments were proposed. In medieval times, homosexuals were burnt at the stake. In many parts of the world homosexuality remains a crime and violence against gay and lesbian people is often ignored or condoned by state authorities.

Since the Wolfenden Report in 1957, and its recommendations for the Sexual Offences Act 1967, there have been no criminal sanctions for consenting adults in private who have reached the age of consent in the UK. Certain issues – such as adoption, sex education and the age of consent itself – have raised concern among the public, and discrimination in these areas has been endorsed by the British government. However, in secular society the law has changed, with same-sex unions now recognised under law in the Civil Partnership Act 2004. Legislation preventing discrimination against people on the basis of sexual orientation have been tightened so that, for instance, Roman Catholic adoption agencies can no longer be funded by the state unless they accept applications from any couple, including gay and lesbian couples.

Christianity, the Bible and homosexuality

Christians have viewed homosexuality as wrong on many levels. There is no possibility of life arising from the sexual union, and so it is wrong on a natural law basis. Some scriptural sources have implied a divine command against homosexuality. In Leviticus (18:22) we find 'Do not lie with a man as one lies with a woman: that is detestable' (New International Version) and it is punishable by death (Leviticus 20:13). Deuteronomy (23:17–18) prohibits temple prostitution, and in Genesis (19:4–11), God destroys Sodom. This story is interpreted as showing God's displeasure with Sodom as resulting from His displeasure with homosexuality. Genesis (2:24) says, 'For this reason a man will leave his father and mother and be united to his wife, and they will become one flesh' (New International Version). This is understood by many Christians as a definition of human relationships in heterosexual terms and is quoted by Jesus in the New Testament (Matthew 19:5 and Mark 10:7) and by St Paul (Ephesians 5:31).

St Paul's letters have influenced Christian teaching on homosexuality. In Romans 1:21–31, St Paul describes people engaging in same-sex sexual acts as 'degrading their bodies' and having 'unnatural relations' and he writes about 'men committing indecent acts with men' (New International Version). In 1 Corinthians 6:9–11, a list of unrighteous kinds of people includes the words *malakoi* and *arsenokoitai*, which have been translated as 'male prostitute' and 'sodomite'. However, these interpretations are disputed. Gareth Moore (1992) argues that St Paul's criticism of homosexual life comes from his assertion that the homosexual lifestyle is a product of a godless people. The existence today of pious homosexual Christians does not fit his reasoning.

Christian Churches, the Bible and homosexuality

The orthodox interpretations of scripture and natural law have led Christian Churches to oppose homosexual sex and sometimes homosexuality itself. The worldwide Anglican community has debated the issue of gay priests and gay marriage and commented that the ordinations of 'practicing homosexuals and the blessing of same sex unions call into question the authority of Holy Scripture' (Religious Tolerance website, www.religioustolerance.org).

In its *Book of Discipline* (1996), the United Methodist Church instructs that:

> Homosexual persons are no less than heterosexual persons … are individuals of sacred worth … Although we do not condone the practice of homosexuality and consider this practice incompatible with Christian teaching.
>
> *United Methodist Church*, 1996

The Roman Catholic Church's teachings on homosexuality are summarised in the *Catechism of the Catholic Church* (1997, paras 2357–59). The Church maintains that there is no sin involved in an inclination towards a member of the same sex, as such an inclination is not freely chosen and is a trial for the person. The homosexual person should be treated with respect, compassion and sensitivity, and unjust discrimination should be avoided. The Church teaches that such people are called to chastity with the help of friendship, prayer and grace to achieve Christian perfection. However, the Church maintains that homosexual acts do not proceed from a 'genuine affective' and sexual complementarity (*Catechism of the Catholic Church*, 1997, para. 2357). The acts are sinful because of the biblical condemnation of homosexual acts as depraved and intrinsically disordered (Congregation for the Doctrine of the Faith, *Persona Humana*, 8). They are, arguably, against natural law.

Others dispute this, suggesting that the unitive act between a loving couple is a good enough purpose for sex, despite being non-reproductive. Many sexual acts – such as sex in the non-fertile part of the menstrual cycle, sex after the menopause, sex when one or both partners are infertile, and sex when the woman is pregnant – cannot lead to reproduction. If we reject the reproductive imperative in sex, then natural law no longer opposes homosexual sex. Kate Saunders and Peter Stamford (1992) note that Jesus said nothing about homosexuality. They note that in 1991, the Polish primate Cardinal Glemp referred to homosexuals as 'backyard mongrels'. Saunders and Stamford suggest statements like this fuel intolerance. Arcigay, an Italian gay rights group, has linked the Church's teaching with violent expressions of intolerance. Arcigay estimates that each year between 150 and 200 gay men are murdered in Italy because of their sexual orientation (Religious Tolerance website, www.religioustolerance.org).

The different approaches to biblical interpretation have led to a fundamental divide in the Anglican Communion. In 2003, in the USA, the New Hampshire diocese chose as bishop an openly gay man, Gene Robinson, who lives with his partner. This act led to a crisis meeting of Anglican archbishops and many statements to the media that such a move could cause a split in the Communion.

Liberal Christian support for homosexuality

Liberal Christian writers challenge the traditional condemnation of homosexuality. They maintain that the quality of the relationship – be it heterosexual or homosexual – is what determines its moral value. The Bible teaches that all are made 'in the image and likeness of God'. If God creates men and women as homosexuals, then that nature and inclination must be good.

■ **Activities**

1 What objections do some Christians have to homosexual sex?

2 What are the criticisms of the traditional Christian natural law and biblical approaches, and how convincing do you think they are?

3 Describe the different approaches to sexual ethics. What are their strengths and weaknesses?

■ Take it further

There is much debate about the issue of homosexuality and ordination in the Anglican Communion. Visit the BBC News website and search their news archive to find out the latest.

■ Key terms

Sages: wise people.

John Boswell (1982) is critical of the use of scripture by opponents of homosexuality. Note that other rules from similar texts are not so emphatically enforced. The Bible condemns hypocrisy and greed, but no one died at the stake in medieval times for these offences, while homosexuals perished. Moore (1992) writes that while Christians are happy to follow the law set out in Leviticus, which says that it is immoral for a man to lie with a man, they reject the passage later on that advocates beheading as a punishment. Christians do not follow the requirement in Leviticus 19:19 that forbids the wearing of garments made of two kinds of material. Moore argues that we are ignoring the laws that we find inconvenient while pursuing those that attack minorities that we do not like (pp184–6). In other words, Scripture is being used inconsistently to reinforce prejudices. Moore argues that there is a Christian basis for an inclusive attitude towards homosexuals, because Christianity is a religion that positively seeks to make room for the marginalised and outcasts in society (1 Corinthians 1:26–28; see the Religious Tolerance website, www.religioustolerance.org).

To produce a Christian ethic that regards homosexual lifestyles as positive and good requires a considerable re-evaluation of Scripture and a change in the assumptions about natural law. It is questionable whether a religion rooted in the heterosexual Hebrew culture, which saw man and woman as made for union with each other, can ever adequately incorporate homosexual marriage and lifestyle. However, Christianity has been able to reject its approval of slavery and its endorsement of female subservience – ideas that also have their roots in ancient Hebrew culture – so perhaps the view on homosexuality can change too. Within most Christian denominations there are active groups of gay, lesbian, bisexual and transsexual Christians who argue this change must happen.

Contemporary Judaism, sex and relationships

Within Judaism there are many different views of sex and relationships and quite distinct stances taken within orthodox and reform Judaism. They echo the pattern found in the sacred texts with, on the one hand, sex linked to relational sensuality and unity, and on the other tensions between sex and holiness. Contrasting ethical perspectives are found between orthodox and reform movements in Judaism.

Hannah Rockman notes that:

> Throughout the Halakhah (Jewish law) the view is held that a loving companionship between husband and wife is a virtue and a duty.

Rockman, 1995

She notes the following general rules that apply to sexual relationships:

■ Sexual relations may take place only between a man and a woman.

■ Sexual relations and marriage are not permitted with someone outside the circle of the Jewish people or inside the circle of close relatives established by the Bible and the **Sages**.

■ Sexual relations are a mitzvah, a religious duty, within a properly covenanted marriage in accordance with Jewish law. Outside of that covenant, premarital sexual relations are not condoned and extramarital relations are considered crimes.

Beyond this there are further prohibitions on sex when intoxicated (in marriage) and sex when a couple are considering separation.

Within marriage itself there are restrictions on sexual activity, notably a restriction on sexual relations with a menstruant woman (*niddah*) which lasts for seven days after the menstrual flow has ceased until a ritual bath has taken place (Leviticus 15:19). These restrictions are aimed at decency or the protection of an unwilling partner.

Solomon (2000) writes that in Judaism, sexual relations outside marriage are forbidden although 'living together' is common in Jewish circles in western countries. He observes that just as there were concubines in the Hebrew Scriptures showing a discrepancy between the rules and how people lived then, so too today we have a discrepancy between traditional rules and contemporary practice with regard to sexual orientation and lifestyle. He observes:

> Biblical and rabbinic law unanimously condemn homosexual practices, but this has not prevented the formation of Jewish 'gay' clubs and even Synagogues.

Solomon, 2000

Early Hebrew law regarded marriage as a purchase and assigned women the lowly status of the husband's property. Arguably this is still the case in Orthodox Judaism. The wife could not own or inherit property herself and divorce was a right that only men could exercise. Greenberg (1991) argues there are quite different attitudes to women in Judaism.

Being born into Judaism means being born into a **covenantal group**. Men have a physical sign of this in circumcision, but thankfully there is no practice of female circumcision. This sign is referred to in prayers, which therefore exclude women, who do not bear the sign. Plaskow argues that women can only hear the message that men carry the sign of covenant as establishing a marginal position in the community (1991, p82). Traditionally the coming of age ceremony for boys is greeted with much ceremony (bar mitzvah); not so the ceremony for girls. Greenberg notes that changes are being made to address some of these inequalities with the development of rituals for girls. Contemporary perspectives on sex and relationships are coloured by ethical debates about the place of women in Judaism.

This patriarchal approach has been rejected by some modern liberal and reformed Jewish views of marriage, which see men and women as equal in the relationship – although, in practice, this equality is not evident in all marriages. Solomon (2000) argues that Judaism is concerned with the marriage relationship which should be based on mutual love, respect and support. Greenberg is critical that it is the man who takes the woman in marriage, implying that the man has the power (1991, p9). It is entered into on a permanent basis, though divorce is permitted but only with the issuing of a get, or bill of divorce, from the husband to the wife in the presence of witnesses. Solomon notes that:

> Orthodox women have often suffered great hardship through this requirement, for little can be done to force a husband to authorize a get if he is unwilling, and the rabbinical courts will not simply 'dissolve' a marriage. Recently, steps have been taken to ameliorate the situation, taking advantage of a variety of legal processes available in different countries.

Solomon, 2000

Key terms

Covenantal group: a group bound by a covenant with God.

Individual Christian and Jewish perspectives

Jack Dominion, the Catholic psychologist, has studied marriage and sexuality in detail and believes that a new definition or description of sex is needed. Taking these recent expressions from the Churches and developing them to take account of contemporary psychology, he writes that sex is a personal expression (1991, pp94–5). It communicates recognition and appreciation between the partners, it confirms the sexual identity of man and woman completely, it brings couples reconciliation and healing after dispute and hurt, it celebrates life and provides profound meaning, and it is a profound way of thanking each other for the loving partnership that they have. The sexual act is a model of total unity between the two people, which reflects the idea of sex in Genesis, restated by Jesus and St Paul. Jack Dominion separates children from this personal expression of love. The personal expression found in sex is present with or without the life-giving dimension.

Jack Dominion believes that Christianity has made a fundamental error by stressing the biological aspect of sex, and that this has had the effect of trivialising the act of sex. Until the 20th century there was no attempt to differentiate between sex as a biological act and making love as a personal expression.

The Catholic, Protestant and Orthodox Churches continue to maintain that sex is a practice exclusively for those who are committed to permanent loving relationships. However, among teenagers it is now far more common, partly due to the availability of more reliable contraception, and more couples are living together before marrying. Such relationships have been traditionally referred to as 'living in sin'. Jack Dominion has observed that where the relationship is committed, loving and permanent, the criteria are met and, arguably, the lifestyle is morally acceptable by traditional Christian standards (Dominion, 1991, pp214–16) – although mainstream Churches reject this view.

Timothy Radcliffe (2008) writes that a Christian sexual ethic can be derived from Jesus' gift of himself in the Last Supper. Rather than beginning with the question 'What is permitted and what is forbidden?', Radcliffe argues that the important questions are 'What does my behaviour say? How does my behaviour affect human communion?'. Jesus expresses his communion with God by giving his body through his sacrifice on the cross. Radcliffe writes:

> When Jesus gave us his body, he was expressing the deepest meaning of what it is to be a body. To be a body is to receive all that this body is from one's parents and their parents before them. It is ultimately to receive one's being from God. Our existence is a gift in every moment. God gives me being now. So our sexual relationship should be expressive of the gift of oneself to another, and the acceptance of the gift which is the being of the other person.

Radcliffe, 2008

In giving ourselves to each other, the gift cannot be a casual gift – here I am now but I will be gone tomorrow, or thanks for the sexual pleasure but I am never going to see you again. Sexual violence is no gift. Sexual love cannot be an exercise in power. Sexuality is founded on the giving and receiving of gifts and at its heart are the attitudes of generosity and gratitude. 'It is the transmission of the gift of our being, and so a profound expression of what it means to be human' (Radcliffe, 2008, p13).

Traditional Judaism faces many challenges in the current age with regard to how it responds to sexual ethics. Arthur Waskow (1995) in his controversial chapter writes that sexual ethics raise extraordinarily puzzling and painful dilemmas in Jewish daily life. While some turn to the traditional Jewish code of sexual behaviour, others find this difficult when facing people's unique and individual situations. He believes there is doubt over sex between unmarried people, people of the same gender and monogamy in marriage. There is a wide divergence between the official sexual ethic of no sex until marriage and the reality of most westerners that sexual awakening happens many years before marriage for the majority of people. He notes that while the emphasis in the commandment to be fruitful and multiply is on reproduction, in the *Song of Songs* there is an emphasis on sensual pleasure and loving companionship. He also argues for a more realistic acceptance of the changes which take place in life patterns in a person's lifetime and that marriage changes greatly during that time as it is exposed to financial burdens. Marriages for younger people, he writes, should be made easier to enter and leave in the early years. He also thinks there should be much greater honesty about the fluidity of sexual relationships among unmarried people, and other Jewish traditions of sexual relationships such as concubines could be looked to once again as forming the basis of a more open but nevertheless recognised sexual relationship.

Waskow's suggestions are radical and attract criticism from conventional religious perspectives. However, his argument that religion should take more seriously its traditions of sensual pleasure and loving companionship rather than exclusively concerning themselves with procreation, seem less easy to dispel.

Patriarchal views of the subservience of women and their role as principally for the raising of children are present in certain religious communities and certain religious understandings which seem at odds to the western idea of the emancipation of women into society.

Muslim approaches to sex, marriage and relationships

Riffat Hassan (1991) argues that sexuality, that is to say the quality of being sexual, is affirmed in the Islamic tradition because human beings are created as sexual beings and differentiated creatures (male and female). Sexuality is not the opposite of spirituality but a sign of God's mercy and bounty.

> And among His [God's] signs
> Is this, that He created
> For you mates from among
> Yourselves, that ye may
> Dwell in tranquillity with them,
> And He has put love
> And mercy between your [hearts]
> Verily in that are signs
> For those who reflect

Qur'an, Surah, 30

Sexuality is not about our animal nature or our material sinfulness, but rather is a divine tool for creating man–woman relationships characterised by togetherness, tranquillity, love and mercy (Hassan, 1991, p97). Men and women are each others' mates and they were created from

Activity

'These individual perspectives just show that some religious believers are abandoning the values of their religion for the values of society.' Do you agree or disagree? Give reasons for your view.

Key terms

Patriarchal views: views that are related to or characteristic of a system of society controlled by men.

Take it further

The Religious Tolerance website has a great deal of information about recent debates associated with marriage and relationships. To research more, see www.religioustolerance.org.

a single source (Surah 53 and 75). There is no tradition of woman being created from man in Islam.

Sexual desire itself is thought by some to be a manifestation of God's wisdom apart from the purpose of procreation.

> when the individual yields to it and satisfies it, he experiences a delight which would be without match if it were lasting. It is a foretaste of the delights secured for men in Paradise, because to make a promise to men of delights they have not tasted would be ineffective

al-Ghazali, in **Mernissi,** *1991*

Sex and sexuality are part of normal married life. The idea that the pleasures of human sexuality provide a foretaste of life after death is a powerful way of giving a sense of sacredness to sexuality. This is a long way from the idea that sex and sexuality are sinful and a link between sexuality and temptations of the flesh. Nevertheless this positive expression of sexuality seems not fully realised for women. While men have a right to have their sexual desires fulfilled by their wives, traditionalists have held that the same is not so for their wives despite the powerful sentiments of equality present in the Qur'an.

Sexual activity is widely held to be the preserve of marriage, and the virginity, especially of women, is frequently held to be of the utmost importance in securing a good marriage. The extent to which these attitudes come from the religion or the culture is not clear. For instance, a number of legal interpretations were applied to unmarried women that seem to be liberal by modern standards.

> In the case of a deserted or widowed woman who becomes pregnant she may be protected by the legal fiction (hila) of the 'sleeping foetus', according to which a pregnancy can be accepted as lasting five or even seven years, while the child remains the legal heir of the dead or absent husband. An unmarried woman who becomes pregnant can resort to the fiction of the 'public bath'. Baths were traditionally opened on alternating days or hours for men and women, and a virgin, it was claimed, who visited the public baths after the men had just vacated them might inadvertently sit on a pool of semen thereby making herself pregnant.

Ruthven, 2000

Unfaithful wives or others accused of illicit sexual relations could incur quite draconian punishments and yet the legal requirement to have four adult witnesses reduces the possibility of actually applying such punishments. Some Muslim countries today use forms of Sharia law which have very severe punishments for sexual crimes, yet at the same time such interpretations seem to ignore many of the Qur'anic principles of equality for women, so it is difficult to know how to interpret such practices.

In marriage Islam has provisions which seem to conflict with the fundamental Judeo-Christian value of monogamy: 'marry such women as seem good to you, two, three, four' (Qur'an, 4:3). This quote shows that the Qur'an permits husbands to take more than one wife. The Prophet himself had at least a dozen wives for much of his life though he was monogamous until he was 53 or 54. Some historians suggest he consummated the union with 14 wives concurrently, though the Prophet had a number of special privileges in this regard that other men do not have and the Qur'an only permits ordinary men one, two, three or four wives (Hekmat, 1997, p128). Since the Qur'an then permits the taking of up to four wives the practice has been widespread, though conditions are attached – the husband must treat those wives with absolute equality.

At the same time the Qur'an affirms a strong sense of equality between men and women:

> Men and women who have surrendered,
> believing men and believing women,
> obedient men and obedient women,
> truthful men and truthful women,
> humble men and humble women,
> men and women who give in charity,
> men who fast and women who fast,
> men and women who guard their private parts,
> men and women who remember God oft –
> for them God has prepared forgiveness and a mighty wage.
>
> *Qur'an, 33:35*

Muslims interpret the Qur'anic rules on polygamy in different ways. On the face of it, the Qur'an seems to suggest an inequality which does not easily match the idea of equality also found in it. Some, such as Jamila Brijbhushan, argue that while it permits polygamy, a man may only take a second or third wife if he treats each wife equally. The introduction of these conditions at the time of the Prophet can be seen as an attempt to reject the existing cultural practices which allowed multiple wives but made few or no provisions for how those wives should be treated. In other words, while it seems to undermine women, it actually raises their status. It should be remembered that within the Qur'an there are many verses which express equality. For instance, women have control over their own property and income, they should have access to the same level of education as men, and so on. The relative treatment of women was improved (Brijbhushan, 1980, p56). Others argue that this is not an adequate answer as it seems to encourage other contemporary practices which deny women's status.

Marriage in Islam is a contractual arrangement rather than a sacrament as in Christianity, and it must be negotiated, though Muslim legal scholars have different opinions about whether women are in an equal position to set terms in such negotiations. Another factor in such negotiations is whether the family of the woman has wealth and power. Unlike Christianity with its virtue of celibacy, all Muslims are encouraged to marry. Husbands have the power to issue a divorce by *talaq*, a unilateral declaration in which he says 'I divorce you' three times. However, there must be a waiting time of three months before the final declaration is made to make sure the woman is not pregnant, and in that time reconciliation may take place. The final declaration makes the divorce. Women do not have this authority as it is men who are considered to be head of the household (Ruthven, 2000, p97).

Another distinctive aspect of Muslim approaches to marriage is the possibility of a temporary marriage contract (*mut'ah* or *sigheh*) signed for a period from a single hour to 99 years, which some argue is an ethically superior model to the free sexual relations of liberal secular society.

The question of patriarchal values which causes difficulty in both Christianity and Judaism is also an issue in Islam, as it questions the idea of equality between men and women. This extract from Fatima Mernissi's book *Women and Islam* (1991) illustrates this:

'Can a women be a leader of Muslims?' I asked my grocer, who like most grocers in Morocco, is a true 'barometer' of public opinion.

'I take refuge in Allah!' he exclaimed, shocked, despite the friendly relations between us. Aghast at the idea, he almost dropped the half dozen eggs I had come to buy.

'May God protect us from the catastrophes of the times!' mumbled a customer who was buying olives, as he made as if to spit. My grocer is a fanatic about cleanliness, and not even denouncing a heresy justifies dirtying the floor in his view.

A second customer, a schoolteacher whom I vaguely knew from the newsstand, stood slowly caressing his wet mint leaves, and then hit me with a Hadith that he knew would be fatal: 'Those who entrust their affairs to a woman will never know prosperity!' Silence fell on the scene. There was nothing I could say. In a Muslim theocracy, a Hadith (tradition), is no small matter. The Hadith collections are works that record in minute detail what the prophet said and did.

Mernissi, 1991

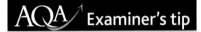

Examiner's tip

Do not worry too much about remembering where specific teachings come from within the Bible/Qur'an/ Guru Granth Sahib (GGS), etc. Examiners only need to know that you are aware of the teachings and are able to quote them accurately. You will not be marked down by saying that something comes from the Old Testament when it comes from the New Testament, but there are certain well-known passages that examiners will expect you to get right (e.g. the Ten Commandments, the Shema, the Shahadah).

This basic attitude to women raises important questions for Islamic understanding of sex and marriage. Fatima Mernissi explores the process of how the *hadiths* were recorded and considers the possibility that some may have reflected more of the culture than the actual words. Her study extends to consider traditions of misogyny found in Arab cultures that influenced the development of Islam. Riffat Hassan (1991) also argues that there are controversies about the authenticity of *hadiths* which has meant that many moderate Muslim scholars are sceptical about them.

The implication is that there is a need for a better understanding of the context in which religion has developed in order to understand apparent conflicts between some of the values found in the Qur'an (as noted above) and later traditions.

■ Hindu approaches to sex, marriage and relationships

In Hinduism, approaches to sex and marriage are complex and diverse. It is difficult to generalise about and religious aspects are difficult to distinguish from non-religious cultural traditions.

Within Hinduism there are traditional class-based ideas that marriage should only exist within the same caste (Brahma marriage) and strong cultural traditions which treat men and women differently, not unlike western traditions prior to the modern era. A son, for instance, can be more highly valued than a daughter. Cybelle Shattuck (1999), writing about the duties accorded to castes, notes that women's lives were not organised into the four castes in the way men's lives were. Female sages are recorded as having taken part in the Upanishadic debates which suggest girls did not go through a student stage in the Vedic age.

Householder life was considered the primary focus for women, so a girl's education was limited to the art of running a home. It is said that the marriage ceremony is a woman's equivalent to the ritual that marks a boy's entry into the formal student stage, serving her husband is like serving a guru (spiritual teacher), and household chores are her fire rituals.

Shattuck, 1999

One consequence of this is that daily worship tends to be the responsibility of the women because it is based within the household. The woman has a leading role in the family dharma where people fulfil all of their religious duties and practise daily devotions.

Shattuck notes some important developments in modern Hinduism despite the patriarchal cultural influences. There are a significant number of women gurus, and in the 19th and 20th centuries reformers have attempted to reach back to what she describes as pure Hindu traditions recorded in the Vedas and the Upanishads.

> In these texts, women were educated in the Vedic lore just like men. Women like Gargi appear in the texts taking part in scholarly debates with the men and acquitting themselves admirably. The reformers used these references as a basis to advocate education for both men and women as a necessary basis for an ideal Hindu society. Furthermore, since in the Vedas women could speak in public forums and spend equal numbers of years in school as men, there was grounds for rejecting social practices like purdah (the seclusion of women), child-marriage, sati, and permanent widowhood. Because of this activism, social organizations of women emerged within both the Arya Samaj and the Brahmo Samaj.

Shattuck, 1999

There have been increased opportunities for women to have religious roles as gurus and temple priests. Patriarchal attitudes to women in Hindu cultures had led to religious protest by women and **dalits**. A Hindu Brahmin, Ram Mohan Roy (1772–1833), wrote against idolatry, **sati**, child-marriage and caste, and also wrote in favour of education for women. He was a social reformer who outraged orthodox Hindus. Kim Knott notes a movement called the Brahma Kumari movement which was founded in the 1930s:

> Brahma Kumaris do not protest vocally against the sexual and physical abuse of women within the family, but they offer an alternative, seeking a gradual transformation of family relationships through yoga and abstention from alcohol and sex.

Knott, 2000

After India achieved independence women were able to make some progress in gaining equality and rights – equality was guaranteed in the Constitution of 1950 though laws against child-marriage and other injustices took longer to secure and there are still such practices in rural parts of India.

In Hinduism, Shattuck writes that marriage is the biggest lifecycle ritual in most people's lives. In marriage two people enter the householder stage, a great transition of responsibility. Marriages are often arranged. A suitable match is sought out by parents using extended family networks.

> Ideally the bride and groom will come from the same area, speak the same language, and be from the same caste. Responsible parents try to find their children partners of similar educational background and good temperament. A girl's family will also take into consideration a groom's potential earning ability to ensure her future security and make sure that he does not have too many younger siblings since his wife may end up working too hard to serve them.

Shattuck, 1999

Link

For more on dharma, see p131 of *AQA Religious Studies: Ethics AS*.

Key terms

Dalits: sometimes called the untouchables, the lowest level of the Indian caste system.

Sati: the immolation of a widow on her husband's funeral pyre.

Reformers such as Dayananda Sarasvati (1824–83) advocated love matches, and campaigned against child-marriages. Love marriages are more common in the modern times although arranged marriages within castes are still common.

This is not the only tradition of marriage found in Hinduism. There is also Taiva marriage 'in which there is no restriction of caste and age, and which is based on the mutual consent (*paraspareccha*) of man and woman' though this is thought to be more of an attempt to reform Hindu laws (Knott, 2000, p67). Marriage traditions are affected by inequality in the treatment of women. Knott notes that sons by tradition support the family, conduct rituals at the death of their parents and also bring wealth into the family at the time of marriage, while daughters are a drain on the family's resources, as the dowry (money and goods) has to be given by her parents to the groom and his family when they marry (p84). Kim Knott's summary of the four stages of life also illustrates the status of women:

> Four stages of life were described in later Hindu texts, though originally they were seen not as stages but as alternative life-choices. Only 'twice-born' males undertook the four ashramas, which were the stages of: student (brahmacharya) householder (grihastha) forest dweller (vanaprastha) renouncer (sannyasa). Following their early years in their father's home, young women were married. Marriage was seen as their rite of initiation into the duties of a wife.

Knott, 2000

Within Hinduism there is the so-called *sex-cult* of Tantra which has come to be an obsession of westerners and is believed to offer hidden secrets for prolonged sexual satisfaction. Tantric texts state that sexual activity can have different functions. It may be procreative, pleasurable or liberating, and it is this last aim that Tantric sex seeks to achieve. In exploring sex in Hinduism some attention must be paid to the enormous interest and impact Tantra has had on the west. Hugh B. Urban notes that it entered western popular imagination in a huge way as entertainers, musicians and poets took an active interest in 'this exotic brand of Eastern spirituality' (Urban, 2003, p224). Some see this liberated religious view of sex as contrasting a sinful idea of sex found in Christianity. However, Urban explains that this in turn has made Tantra just as sex obsessed as the west.

> these Tantric masters have been influenced by Western ideas and obsessions—perhaps above all, the preoccupation with sex and its liberation

Urban, 2003

While Tantra seems to offer the possibility of satisfying a powerful desire within western society, the inequalities found in sex selection and sex determination contrast with values of equality. According to Shattuck there are actually very few Tantric groups in south-east Asia and many of these groups practise Tantra symbolically rather than physically.

■ Buddhist approaches to sex, marriage and relationships

Damien Keown suggests that Buddhism and Christianity have much in common in the area of sexuality though at first there are some apparent differences with Christian hangups about virginity and celibacy set against more relaxed Buddhist attitudes (Keown, 2005, p53). However, Keown argues that Buddhism is much more conservative and reserved than westerners might think.

Sacred texts prohibit monks from speaking to women about obscene or erotic acts despite the traditions or Tantric erotic art. Buddhism does not require or expect procreation, unlike biblical teachings, as birth is a gateway to a life of suffering. Making babies is not part of a divine plan, though the birth of babies is considered to be a precious event.

Keown argues that as Buddhism is an **ascetic tradition**, it is naturally suspicious of desire and sexual desire has its dangers. Cravings cause suffering and erotic cravings can be incredibly strong. Buddha said that nothing can overpower a man's mind as much as 'the form of a woman' (A.iii.68f). Women arouse men: 'Lord, how should we behave towards women? – Do not see them, Ananda' (D.ii.141, in Keown, 2005, p55).

For some, this shows a misogynistic streak in Buddhism, but Keown argues that these words are there to protect a celibate community of monks. Also, it is the desire that is the problem, not that which is desired.

Marriage is recommended to those who cannot live celibate lives, but it is not a sacrament and ceremonies are not presided over by monks according to Keown (though some Japanese Buddhist priets do preside). Traditionally there is no marriage service, but the increasing western interest in Buddhism has led to Buddhist versions of Christian marriage ceremonies.

Early Buddhist texts offer guidance for husbands and wives:

> 'In five ways should a wife … be ministered to by her husband: by respect, by courtesy, by faithfulness, by giving her authority (in the home), by providing her with adornments.' and for the wife 'her duties are well performed, she shows hospitality to the kin of both, is faithful, watches over the goods he (her husband) brings, and shows skill and artistry in discharging all her business'.

*Buddhist Publication Society, 1985, in **Keown**, 2005*

Keown argues that though monogamy is preferred, there is a lot of local diversity including temporary and permanent arrangements due to cultural rather than religious differences. There is a sense that the lay (i.e. ordinary) married way of life is not as spiritual as the celibate monastic way of life, but it is appropriate for those who have not been able to wean themselves off their material desires yet. Keown writes that with the exception of some examples in Japan:

> The Buddhist ideal has always been to abandon family life, subdue sexual desire, and live either alone, or in a celibate community. In this respect, the Buddha provides the perfect role model: at the age of 29 he turned his back on family life and remained celibate for the rest of his days.

Keown, 2005

Sexual moral behaviour is governed by the third precept which prohibits sexual misconduct, mainly adultery. Relationships should be honest, informed by right speech, action and livelihood. Cheating on a spouse is very clearly none of these things. There are also prohibitions against marrying very young girls and marrying close relatives, and it is assumed that sex is for marriage only. The teachings prohibiting harm include

Key terms

Ascetic tradition: describes a lifestyle characterised by abstinence from various sorts of worldly pleasures.

both physical and emotional harm and apply to sexual crimes such as rape or harassment.

Early Buddhist commentaries also prohibit certain other sexual conduct including sex in public places, or through a 'forbidden orifice' or at times unsuitable for the woman (Keown, p60).

Tensions exist in Buddhism over the issue of homosexuality, as they do in other religions. There is no direct discussion in the early sources of Buddhism apart from in terms of monastic lifestyle, where it is prohibited. A group of people are excluded from joining monastic orders and they are described as *pandakas*, thought to refer to 'sexually dysfunctional passive homosexuals' according to Peter Harvey (2000).

There have been modern calls to expel gay Buddhist monks from monasteries. The Dalai Lama has stipulated that homosexual men and women have dignity and rights, but masturbation, oral and anal sex are all improper uses of organs. He has also said that Buddhism takes account of time and culture and so in theory homosexual sex could become acceptable but no single teacher can redefine existing precepts – it must be done on a collective level from within the sangha.

Keown argues that homosexual ethics in Buddhism reveal tensions between absolute and relative views of the precepts. On the one hand there is the possibility that Buddhism might change its teaching on this matter, but if this is so then does that also apply to any other precept?

Keown argues that it is strange that Buddhism places no obligation on reproduction while at the same time regulating sexual practices by examining whether sexual organs are being used for procreative purposes. Like Christianity, celibacy is preferred and then, if not celibacy, married procreative sex.

Harvey has surveyed Buddhist culture and his study reveals that while some cultures view homosexuality in a very negative light, there are also signs of change. For instance, Harvey notes that the Friends of the Western Buddhist Order welcomes homosexuals in its outreach programmes and runs a meditation retreat for gay and lesbian Buddhists. Their view is that homosexuality, heterosexuality and transvestitism are all morally neutral – it is sexuality in general terms which to some extent must be transcended. Sexuality is only a peripheral aspect of the human person, but at the same time celibacy should not be chosen because of a fear of sexuality (Harvey, 2000, pp428–9).

Thus within Buddhism there is a broad range of responses towards western values of tolerance in matters of sexual diversity.

Sikh approaches to sex, marriage and relationships

Morgan and Lawton (1996) write that in Sikh teaching family responsibilities and self-restraint are very important: 'Marriage is a spiritual union, not only the union of two bodies' (p105). In Sikhism, arranged marriage is the norm, many members of the family should support a proposed marriage and the marriage is a union between two families. However, the couple must agree and there should be no coercion. The Gurus were critical of the Indian dowry system though it still features in marriage arrangements. Marriage is of such importance that it should take place in the presence of the Guru Granth Sahib. Marriages are often arranged before puberty.

Morgan and Lawton note that the honour (*izzat*) of an extended family is affected by the individual conduct of one member of the family and the honour of a girl is particularly important. Girls should not behave without decent modesty. Sex before marriage is completely out of the question and activities which might lead to this are discouraged, as indicated by interviews with British Sikh parents:

> There is no courting. Our grown-up girls don't generally go to discos and parties.
>
> *Bowker, 1983*

Morgan and Lawton (1996) note that boys do not have such strict requirements placed on them. Cole writes that 'boys have more freedom as they grow older but teenage girls are not allowed to go out unchaperoned' (Cole, 2004, p313).

Morgan and Lawton also comment that there is no Sikh writing on homosexuality (their book was written in 1996), though men and women are expected to marry members of the opposite sex and have children – heterosexuality is the norm. Marriage is held in very high regard by the Sikh Gurus (who themselves enter matrimony). It is more than a civil ceremony but represents an ideal state for the fusing of 'two souls into one so that they may become spiritually inseparable' (p107).

> They are not husband and wife
> Who only dwell together.
> Only they who have one spirit in two bodies
> Can be called husband and wife.
>
> *Ādi Granth, 1469–1708, Chapter 788*

As such adultery is prohibited, 'Do not cast your eyes on the beauty of another's wife' (*Ādi Granth*, Chapter 274) and the Sikh underwear (*kachh*) is a reminder of the need for marital fidelity. Divorce is rare, though there are situations where it should take place. Mansukhani writes:

> Generally grounds like cruelty, adultery, change of religion, suffering from an incurable disease and in some cases incompatibility of temperaments are accepted by courts for purposes of divorce.
>
> *Mansukhani, 1986*

Non-religious approaches to sexuality

The libertarian approach to sexuality

'Sex' is one of the most searched for words on the internet, and it finds itself on the cover of many magazines. It is not unreasonable to say that the people of the 21st century are obsessed with sex. The ethic that underlies this presentation of sex is a libertarian one. This is the view that sex is morally permissible if there is mutual agreement or consent between the participating parties. This view is sometimes known as a *contractarian* view. There is no need to link sex either to marriage or, specifically, to reproduction, because there is no special traditional or religious view of the function of sex. Human freedom and autonomy are the most important principles or values.

Libertarianism does not allow for sexual crimes such as rape, as they go against the freedom principle – the rape victim is forced to have sex against his or her will. Libertarianism does not allow for sex with minors (children) as they cannot be truly said to have free will – they do not have

---

AQA Examiner's tip

You can study views from more than one religion for this topic, but watch for the wording of the question. If the question specifies that answers should come from *one* religion, then you are wasting your time if you write about more than one. If the question asks for 'a religious perspective', you can write about more than one religion.

Activity

What similarities and differences exist between Hindu, Buddhist and Sikh approaches to sex, marriage and relationships?

the ability to give informed consent. Sex involving any form of deception is also out of the question, as free choices cannot be made if one party is kept in ignorance of issues that might be important.

Libertarians may also adopt the 'harm principle' in their approach to sexuality. To observe the harm principle is to ensure that no harm is done to either party or to other third parties. This is an extension of the libertarian view of freedom. I am allowed as much freedom as possible, without infringing other people's right to freedom, including freedom from harm. I may choose to do as I freely please, but if my actions impinge the freedom of another through the effects that they have on another, then my actions are called into question. If I like you and you like me, and we both want to have sex, then we can as long as we do not harm each other or anyone else. If the sex is adulterous and the betrayed spouse finds out and is harmed, then the act is called into question.

In the libertarian view, what is done in sex is again up to the individuals. There are no restrictions on the kind of sexual activity, no requirement to avoid sexual acts that do not lead to reproduction and so no prohibition of the use of contraception.

There are a number of advantages in the libertarian approach to sexuality. The view celebrates sexual liberation. It allows consenting adults to do as they please. Freedom is a basic principle that is highly regarded in today's society, particularly after centuries in which patriarchal traditions gave women subservient roles in marriage, and religion prescribed and enforced moral laws such as the prohibition of homosexual sex. Libertarianism seems more tolerant and permissive of different sexual activities and lifestyles.

One weakness with libertarian approaches to sexuality regards free consent. It may be argued that adults can make free choices about sex, but what happens when there is an imbalance within the relationship? Consider the boss who makes unwanted advances to the secretary. Quitting the job may not help, as money is needed for dependents, and any reference written by the harasser may well be prejudiced. True freedom may not be present in relationships in which power is not equally distributed between the parties. Belliotti (1991) tells us about Rocco, a poor but honest barber's son who has a family in desperate need of money. His neighbour Vito has an unusual hobby of collecting people's middle fingers in exchange for $5,000 and private medical care. Rocco agrees to have his middle finger chopped off and gets the money in return. Belliotti comments that Rocco's finger is treated as a commodity. He notes that although Rocco agreed to the procedure, there seems to be an important moral dimension that libertarianism cannot account for (pp320–1).

Feminist approaches to sexuality

Feminists criticise both the traditional religious approaches to sexuality and the liberal ones. Most religious approaches rest on a defined cultural role for women, that of the child-bearer, wife and submissive companion. For instance, implicit in the Christian approach is the Hebrew view of women as being created for the man, the property of the man, and in all senses secondary to the man. The defined socially constructed role of mother and wife effectively disempowers women by restricting their status in society and socialising them to meet the desires of men. Christianity relies on natural law and human nature, as do other religions – but this is the product of social conditioning, not nature. The result of this cultural background has been to give women a secondary role in society. The Hebrew and Greek view of women has meant that for hundreds of years they have had little access to politics or wealth, and very little free choice. This situation has affected sexual relationships. Sexual behaviour assumes male dominance and female submission. Most sexual crimes are committed against women. Marriage laws have only recently given equal status to women. Ultra Orthodox Jews today maintain that a divorce is only possible if the husband issues the 'Get' (the contract of divorce) and many women have found themselves locked into marriages, leaving them unable to remarry in the Faith. In some Protestant Christian Churches, the role of women is limited to that of homemaker and child-raiser.

Liberal approaches to sexuality are criticised by feminists because they assume a level playing field. They assume that men and women are in a position to enter freely into a sexual relationship. In a society that is patriarchal, that freedom is questionable. Just as there is an immorality in Rocco having to cut off his finger, so feminists argue that there is an immorality if a women has sex in the setting of an imbalanced social status or a culturally defined role. Women may be so conditioned that they are not even aware of their disempowered status.

An imbalance of immorality?

Some feminists, such as Catharine Mackinnon (1987), argue that sexuality must be re-imagined and remade before moral sexual relationships become possible. Until this is done, sexual activity will be immoral. More extreme feminists, such as Jill Johnston (1974), argue for separation of men and women, and for sex among women as a political statement to undermine the domination and power of men. Mary Daly has argued that women cannot call God father – 'If God is male, then male is God'. If God is seen in male terms then a woman is not fully in the image of God (Daly, 1974). Because of the influence the ancient world has had on Jewish and Christian doctrine (and indeed Islam), some feminists argue that these religions are irredeemably sexist. In the words of Daphne Hampson (1990), since the Enlightenment there has been an ill fit between Christianity and modern thought. The idea of equality does not fit the theology of these religious traditions and so they must be discarded.

Activity

Choose two religions and identify five features in each religion which contrast directly with libertarianism or feminism in their approaches to sex and relationships.

In your view, which provides the most convincing assessment of sexuality and why?

Take it further

Read more about Mary Daly in her article, 'After the death of God the Father: Women's liberation and the transformation of Christian consciousness' at http://scriptorium. lib.duke.edu/wlm/after/. It was originally published in the journal *Commonweal*, 12 March 1971.

Raymond Bellioti rejects the feminist idea that women are incapable of deciding for themselves. If women are indeed too socially conditioned to freely enter into relationships, then this is a justification for paternalism. He does not see a problem with a woman accepting a socially defined role if she chooses it. He also challenges the assumption that sexuality is fundamental to the human person, and therefore as significant as feminists argue (Belliotti, 1991, pp324–5).

■ Issues arising

Is religious teaching relevant to people today?

It certainly seems that the values of modern western society are a long way from those of religion. Religion, for the most part, seems to suggest that sex before marriage is wrong, that many particular kinds of sexual act are wrong if they are not directly related to reproduction, and that many types of sexual relationships are wrong, such as gay and lesbian relationships. Modern liberal western society seems to challenge each of these things with a basic idea that as long as people consent to what is going on, and no one else is harmed, they are fine.

It is possible to argue that religion essentially offers an old-fashioned pre-scientific view of the world which has none of the advantages of modern ideas of human physiology and political ideas of human equality. According to this view, religion is quite simply wrong about its view of the world and has nothing to offer people in the modern world.

A reverse way of working this argument is to say that religion holds truths which have been lost to society today. Modern permissive sexual activity has led to a lot of unhappiness, left people with dysfunctional relationships, left more people living alone than ever before and helped to spread disease. Perhaps a religious perspective would be very relevant to people today. Religious perspectives just seem irrelevant because the ideas within them do not appear to match what a lot of people take for granted in the modern world. Alternatively, perhaps the modern ideas of equality and freedom are important and tell us we need to change some religious perspectives that do not treat women fairly.

More subtle arguments can be made about the differences within religious traditions, contrasting more liberal attitudes towards some of these sexual ethical issues with conservative religious expressions of life.

Should religion concern itself with sexual behaviour?

The image of a minister in a pulpit speaking about sexual acts which are sinful and reproaching the state of things today as regards sex leads to different reactions. For some this is religion playing an important role in holding society to account. For others this is religion encroaching too far into their personal and private lives. Both views might have some truth.

If religion is about how people actually live as opposed to simply what people believe or think, then to ignore sexuality is to ignore a fundamental aspect of human beings. Our sexuality is not simply about acts or even relationships with others, but an essential part of our humanity. For religion to be of relevance it cannot ignore human sexuality. Religions are concerned with human nature. They express ideas about how human beings are and how they should be. They hold messages for humanity about how to live and reach salvation or enlightenment. If how we live affects our progress towards these goals and if sexuality affects how we live, then religion must remain concerned with sex.

Nevertheless, religion sometimes seems rather too concerned with sexual acts. Religion can seem to be an unlikely place to find authority and wisdom in matters of sexuality in light of the problem of sexual abuse in the clergy, for instance, or the treatment of women in some traditions. In modern liberal society people live much more diverse lives. Individuals are able to live in ways which in the past would have meant they were criminalised or expelled from society. Questions remain about the extent to which responsibility for how people live should be held by individuals as opposed to religious authorities.

However, it is not just a matter of differing values, but also new understandings about sexuality. Sexuality seems to be less fixed and less standard for all human beings than was once thought and much more is known about human sexuality than in the past. Many religions teach that sex should be in accordance with certain ideas of what is natural – for instance for procreative reasons. Masturbation is often said to be wrong. However, many women never reach orgasm through simple penetrative sex but are much more likely to do so through masturbation. Modern understandings challenge ideas about what is natural in sex.

Is modern society setting its own codes of behaviour?

It sometimes seems as if there is a deepening gap between the way modern society lives and the way religions suggest people should live. Younger and younger people engage in sexual relationships; sexual acts which were once considered taboo become more commonly accepted in general among consenting adults; and people are able to live lifestyles in which they may have sexual partnerships with a number of others, sometimes simultaneously but more often one after another, as opposed to being with a single person for life. Indeed in modern British society, gay and lesbian relationships have legal recognition in civil partnerships, a far cry to half a century ago when gay sex was criminal. Religion no longer sets moral codes which society accepts. Within religion, liberal voices argue for more tolerance of sexual diversity, more acceptance for instance of gay and lesbian lifestyles. Is religion trying to catch up with the modern morals of society?

One of the most important questions for religion in the modern world is the extent to which it engages with the modern ideas of equality.

The growth of the idea of individual freedom and equality under the law means that religious views of marriage and sex which do not recognise equality between men and women, or do not appreciate diversity when it comes to sexual orientation, seem out of place.

◼ Chapter summary

Religion and love

- Love is understood to have different meanings within and between the different religious traditions, with erotic, compassionate and familial versions.

Sex and relationships

- Different religious traditions have different views of sex and relationships, and issues related to the status of women and the role of reproduction are especially important.

Ancient and modern attitudes to sex and marriage

■ Dualists divide the world into the spiritual and the physical. Some prefer the spiritual over the physical while others celebrate the physical and bemoan the spiritual.

■ There are both positive and negative attitudes to sex in ancient religious traditions.

■ Modern attitudes to sex are more permissive, with greater freedom for sex, and higher status placed on sex.

■ There are serious concerns about the break-up of relationships, STDs and a dissatisfaction with the contemporary sexual climate.

■ Several forces for change affect religious perspectives: the status of women, the availability of safe contraception and new understandings about sexual identity.

Jewish and Christian approaches to sex and relationships

Sacred scripture

■ Sex is depicted in different ways in the Bible, with crimes of sex and positive reflections of sensual aspects of love.

■ Sexuality is God-given and understood in terms of relationships and the uniting of man and woman.

■ The Bible has an example of great eroticism within a context of the unity of man and woman in the *Song of Songs*.

■ The Bible also contains examples of a division between holiness and sexuality illustrated in the rules regarding priests and sex.

■ Celibacy in the New Testament is sometimes represented as a more holy state.

■ Jesus associated with sexual sinners.

The Christian Church and sex and relationships

■ Some ancient Christian writers depict sex in a negative light and see it is a cause of their sin.

■ The religious orders and priesthood in Catholic Christianity are celibate, while Orthodox and Protestant Churches see priesthood as compatible with marriage.

■ Modern Catholic thinking rejects the old dualistic ideas that saw body as bad and soul as good. The human person combines both.

■ Procreation and unity is the purpose of marriage in Christian thinking. The Catholic Church teaches that both elements must always be present in sex. Other Churches do not.

■ Love, sex and marriage are bound together in Christian thinking.

■ Homosexual love is now recognised in UK law as a valid form of union recognised in civil partnerships, although it remains criminal in some parts of the world.

■ The Bible has many texts which some Churches and Christians use to condemn homosexuality, though other Churches and Christians interpret and use those texts differently.

■ Some Churches allow homosexual priests and there are debates in the Anglican Communion about homosexual bishops.

■ The Roman Catholic Church does not condemn homosexuality but does prohibit homosexual sex.

- Christian Churches have been accused of inciting hatred against gay and lesbian people.

- Some liberal Christians dispute traditional views of homosexuality and accuse conservative Christians of using religion to justify prejudice and hatred. They argue for a broader understanding of the union of people in sex.

Contemporary Judaism and sex and relationships

- Differences exist between and within reform, liberal, orthodox and conservative perspectives of sex and relationships.

- Sex outside marriage is prohibited and homosexual sex is condemned, though the Bible has examples of concubinage, and Jewish gay clubs and synagogues exist.

- Rules concerning menstruation restrict sex within marriage.

- Women have traditionally had a low status in marriage and this remains the case in more orthodox Judaism.

- Liberal and reform movements in Judaism reject the patriarchal approach and embrace equality.

Individual Christian and Jewish perspectives

- Jack Dominion believes that Christianity has made a fundamental error by stressing the biological aspect of sex.

- Dominion argues that sex communicates recognition and appreciation, it confirms the sexual identity of man and woman completely, it brings couples reconciliation and healing, it celebrates life and provides profound meaning to the couple's lives.

- Though living together was traditionally called 'living in sin', Dominion argues that where the relationship is committed, loving and permanent the lifestyle is morally acceptable by traditional Christian standards.

- Timothy Radcliffe writes that a Christian sexual ethic can be derived from Jesus' gift of himself at the Last Supper. Jesus expresses his communion with God by giving his body through his sacrifice on the cross. In giving ourselves to each other, the gift cannot be a casual gift.

- Arthur Waskow argues that reproduction has been given more attention than sensual pleasure despite the *Song of Songs*. He argues for a realistic acceptance of the changes in modern life. Marriages for younger people should be made easier to enter and leave in the early years, there should be much greater honesty about the fluidity of sexual relationships among unmarried people.

Muslim approaches to sex, marriage and relationships

- Sexuality is affirmed because human beings are created as sexual beings by God. Sexuality is a divine tool for togetherness; love and mercy and desire are part of God's procreative purpose.

- Sex is a foretaste of life after death. It is the preserve of marriage and some Muslim countries apply severe punishments for sex crimes.

- Men living in Muslim countries may be permitted to take more than one wife as long as all are treated equally.

- All Muslims are encouraged to marry and it is a contract. Husbands have the power of divorce.

- There are traditions of temporary marriage.

■ Some argue that there is a lack of equality in Islam because it has adopted patriarchal traditions in its development that it now needs to set aside.

Hindu approaches to sex, marriage and relationships

■ There are many different views of sex and marriage in Hinduism.

■ Women have a central role in overseeing household religious duties, although they have been excluded from education and positions of authority in religion.

■ This patriarchal treatment of women contrasts the ancient status of women in the Vedas and Upanishads which show women having a greater status.

■ Many reform movements have attempted to change social attitudes to women.

■ While marriage is traditionally arranged and within castes, reformers have argued for love marriages irrespective of caste.

■ Tantra is often misunderstood and misrepresented: it sees liberation as a possible outcome of sex, though in practice there are few Tantra communities.

Buddhist approaches to sex, marriage and relationships

■ Buddhism is reserved and conservative in its attitudes to sex and relationships.

■ While the birth of babies is a precious event, reproduction is not part of a divine plan.

■ Some traditions have seen women as a cause of desires distracting celibate monks.

■ Marriage is recommended for those who cannot live celibate lives, and it should be honest and faithful.

■ Some Buddhists oppose homosexuality and homosexual sex on the grounds that it is unnatural, while others see it as morally neutral.

Sikh approaches to sex, marriage and relationships

■ Marriage is a spiritual union, not only the union of two bodies.

■ The Gurus were critical of the Indian dowry system.

■ Sex before marriage is completely out of the question and activities which might lead to this are discouraged.

■ Heterosexuality is the norm and adultery is prohibited.

Non-religious approaches to sexuality

Libertarian approaches

■ Sex is morally permissible if there is mutual agreement or consent between the participating parties as long as there is no harm done.

■ Sexual crimes such as rape go against the freedom principle.

■ There are no restrictions on the kind of sexual activity – the view celebrates sexual liberation.

■ One weakness with libertarian approaches to sexuality regards free consent. Hypothetically, adults can make free choices about sex, but if there is an imbalance of power within the relationship the choice is not free.

Feminist approaches to sexuality

- Religious approaches rest on a defined cultural role for women, that of the child-bearer, wife and submissive companion, which disempowers women by restricting their status in society and socialising them to meet the desires of men.

- Sexual behaviour assumes male dominance and female submission.

- Liberal approaches to sexuality are criticised by feminists because they assume a level playing field.

- Sexuality must be re-imagined and remade before moral sexual relationships become possible. Until this is done, sexual activity will be immoral.

- Some feminists have argued for the separation of men and women and for sex among women as a political statement to undermine the domination and power of men.

Further reading

Belliotti, R. 'A Sex' in Singer, P. (ed.) *A Companion to Ethics*, Blackwell, 1997, pp315–27. Belliotti's article briefly reviews the historical background and the main arguments and theories surrounding what might be meant by ethical sex.

Hampson, D. *Theology and Feminism*, Blackwell, 1990. This is her thesis that since the Enlightenment there has been an ill fit between Christianity and modern thought on women.

Lafollette, H. 'Personal Relationships' in Singer, P. (ed.) *A Companion to Ethics*, Blackwell, 1997, pp327–32. Lafollette explores some of the interesting conflicts between conventional ethical thinking and common thinking about relationships.

In this chapter you have:

- identified the main approaches to issues of sexuality and relationships by different religious traditions

- explored differences that exist within traditions

- explored the role of sacred texts, institutions and also individual responses in religious approaches to issues of sexuality and relationships

- considered libertarian and feminist approaches to sexual ethics

- considered strengths and weaknesses of religious approaches to issues of sexuality and relationships.

4 Science and technology

By the end of this chapter you will be able to:

- recognise important issues related to science, technology and ethics

- identify different views on related ethical issues in connection with the question of ethical controls, the beneficiaries of technological breakthroughs and aspects of human rights and surveillance, data storage and cyber crime

- describe different aspects of the relationship between religion and science, and issues arising from the ethics of science and technology.

Key questions

1 What should the relationship be between ethics and science?
2 Should one control the other, and if so which should control which?
3 What kinds of ethical rules should science and technology follow and who should keep check?

Activities

Consider what each of these quotations means. Are there any that you strongly agree or disagree with? How might you respond to them?

- 'Science has taught us how to put the atom to work. But to make it work for good instead of for evil lies in the domain dealing with the principles of human duty. We are now facing a problem more of ethics than physics.' (*Baruch, in **Gaither**, 2000, pp47–8*)

- 'Ethics and Science need to shake hands.' (*Cabot, in **Gaither**, 2000, pp47–8*)

- 'Science should submit to ethics, not ethics to science.' (*Gragam, in **Gaither**, 2000, pp47–8*)

- 'Science, by itself, cannot supply us with an ethic. It can show us how to achieve a given end, and it may show us that some ends cannot be achieved.' (*Russell, in **Gaither**, 2000, pp47–8*)

- 'Science cannot stop while ethics catches up … and nobody should expect scientists to do all the thinking for the country.' (*Stackman, in **Gaither**, 2000, pp47–8*)

Ethical decision making in experimentation

Human experimentation

In the last century there have been enormous breakthroughs in medicine. The discovery of penicillin (attributed to Scottish scientist Sir Alexander Fleming) and the mass production of the drug had a major impact on reducing the number of deaths during World War II, perhaps as many as 15 per cent of all casualties among Allied armed forces.

Some terrible mistakes have been made when drug treatments have gone badly wrong such as with **thalidomide**. Testing was inadequate, resulting in terrible effects on the children of women who had taken the drug during their pregnancies. Approximately 10,000 children were born with severe malformities including **phocomelia**. Because of cases such as the thalidomide catastrophe, regulations require new drugs to be tested on both animals and consenting humans (though in the UK children are excluded and cannot be used for these tests). There is some risk, which is one reason why testing on animals is carried out before human trials can begin. Nevertheless, there are recent examples where things have gone wrong. On 13 March 2006, six healthy men were injected with an anti-inflammatory drug being developed for the treatment of rheumatoid arthritis and leukaemia. Almost immediately their bodies swelled up and

Key terms

Thalidomide: a drug prescribed from 1957 to 1961 in many countries chiefly to pregnant women to combat morning sickness.

Phocomelia: a deformity whereby the individual has very short or absent limbs.

Phocomelia is one of the effects of thalidomide

their breathing became erratic. Their organs began to fail leaving two of them in a critical condition. The drug was being developed by a German firm TeGenero. The men had been paid £2,000 each for taking part in the trial.

A number of ethical issues are involved here. First of all there is the duty of doctors, scientists and researchers to act ethically in the production of new drugs, both in their preparation and also in their testing and the open and honest publication of the results. Doctors have traditionally taken an oath, which begins 'first do not harm'. They have a professional ethical duty to the public, their patients, those involved in the production of new medicines and the profession. If a doctor or drug company knows of side-effects to their drugs these must be published. Concealing such information sacrifices the interest of patients or the public for short-term sales goals, and it endangers future medicine production by casting doubt on the integrity of the industry.

These pharmaceutical companies fund the development of new treatments which bring benefit to many. In a recent case GlaxoSmithKline was warned by the UK drugs regulator that they should have been quicker to raise the alarm on the risk of suicidal behaviour associated with the antidepressant Seroxat in those under 18. There was evidence that the drug was not as effective with children and adolescents and evidence that there was a higher risk of suicidal behaviour for those in this age group. While GlaxoSmithKline believed they had published the information early enough the regulator disagreed. It is not known how many young people may have committed suicide as a result of the delay, but the regulator feels many young people were put at unnecessary risk. GlaxoSmithKline is thought to have first known about the risk in the late 1990s, but data showed that details of this risk were not passed to the regulatory authority until May 2003.

Second, the state has an ethical obligation to have a regulated environment requiring safeguards to protect the public from possible side-effects from new drugs while at the same time allowing for the development of new medicines which have life-saving or life-enhancing consequences.

Animal and human testing

For both of the reasons mentioned above, animal and human testing form part of the process involved in gaining a licence to sell a medicine in developed countries. The human testers have to give their informed consent in order for such testing to be ethical. In the past there have been instances where people were unknowing guinea pigs. For instance, soldiers were exposed to levels of radiation during nuclear testing in the South Pacific Ocean which later led to serious medical conditions including cancer. In some cases governments have had to set up compensation schemes for soldiers and civilians affected by radiation.

These ethical questions also affect other forms of medical treatment including surgery. During World War II at the Queen Victoria Hospital near East Grinstead, badly burnt pilots were subject to experimental practices which led to breakthroughs in the treatment of burns and plastic surgery. The pilots who were treated there were known as the Guinea Pig Club and they still meet there once a year. For these pilots and their doctors the risks were unknown, but the consequences of not trying to develop new treatments were very severe indeed so it was a risk worth taking. In times of war, there are occasions where life-saving new ideas have to be tried out and there is no time for testing and slow gradual development. That is one reason why medical breakthroughs often happen during times of war.

In the case of human experimentation, the idea of informed consent seems crucial. Being forced to undergo risky unproven techniques or procedures seems to go against the idea of individual liberty and freedom. It goes against the idea that human beings have a dignity or worth which cannot be removed or ignored. This idea of the dignity of the human person is found in religious traditions where human beings are said to be sacred, and in philosophical traditions such as Kantian ethics which gives human beings value above all other creatures – a value which has no price, even for the greater good, in utilitarian terms.

The idea that procedures should be tested before becoming widely available is vital, so the solution is to invite testers to give informed consent with the promise of further treatment and support if the test goes wrong. Medical procedures and treatments need to be practised first, and established as safe by testing on human beings. This is part of the responsibility that doctors and the government regulatory authorities have to individual patients and the general public. If there are doubts about the integrity or safety of the medical system then there is a real danger to public health. If members of the public cannot trust the treatments being suggested then they may do themselves more harm by not being treated or pursuing an unsafe treatment.

Embryo experimentation

A general starting point for an ethical argument for embryo research is that you should not use embryos for research unless there is a good reason to do so. For instance there is an argument that animals are not a completely suitable subject for testing due to differences between the species. If this is a significant risk then perhaps there is an argument for using embryos in this situation. We can also ask about the nature of the research being undertaken. It is often difficult for all outcomes to be known at the outset of research. You do not know what you are going to find until you have done the research. Generally speaking, in ethical

Activities

1 Should prisoners convicted of serious crimes be required to undergo medical testing as part of giving something back to society?

2 What responsibilities do commercial pharmaceutical companies have to the wider community, doctors and patients?

3 How could it be argued that human testing:

   a undermines human dignity?

   b maintains human dignity?

arguments for embryo research it is argued that **embryo experimentation** has the potential to find cures for serious illnesses by using tissue or cells from embryos. It is possible that such work might help with the treatment of those with Alzheimer's disease, Huntington's disease, diabetes and Parkinson's disease.

This potential has led to increasing pressure to extend what is permissible in embryo research and experimentation. IVF (in vitro fertilisation) itself is underpinned by such research and would not be possible without it. Recently, politicians in the UK voted to extend the research done on human embryos to allow stem cells to be taken from embryos at a very early stage of development, in the hope that this may lead to radical improvements in the treatment of a number of **degenerative diseases**.

There are legal limits to embryo experimentation. A number of practices are prohibited in the UK, including keeping an embryo past the appearance of the primitive streak at about 14 days, placing a human embryo in an animal, replacing the nucleus of a cell of an embryo with the nucleus of another person (human cloning), and altering the genetic structure of any cell while it forms part of an embryo. Note that the primitive streak is a thickening in the surface of the embryo and that it results in the first stages of embryonic development (Human Fertilisation and Embryology Authority (HFEA), 2003, p3).

Two recent developments have brought embryo research into the public arena again: firstly the development of stem cell research and secondly the development of human-animal **cybrid embryos**.

Embryonic stem cells are thought by scientists to be particularly valuable because of their regenerative and indeed generative capacity. For example, in 2005, embryonic stem cells were used to heal broken spines in rats (*Medical News Today*, 2005). Research in 2007 has indicated that it may be possible to reverse age-related muscle degeneration which has caused 14 million people in Europe to become blind. Scientists believe that within five years a treatment will have been developed to cure these people of their blindness (*Metro*, 2007).

Scientists believe that in a relatively short period of time, embryonic stem cell research is already showing benefits that could soon provide important treatments for many people who are currently suffering. While it is sometimes claimed that adult stem cells may provide cures, thus avoiding the need to use human embryos (adult stem cells can be extracted without harming the adult person), many scientists believe that they will not offer such solutions.

A Bill passing through Parliament in May 2008 supported the creation of human-animal cybrid embryos. This involved the insertion of a nucleus of a human cell inside a hollowed-out cow ovum. Scientists again believe that through a better understanding of the development of embryos at the molecular level new treatments for degenerative diseases such as Parkinson's, Alzheimer's and motor neurone disease will be developed.

Key terms

Embryo experimentation: a term that can cause confusion. For the sake of this chapter, what is being referred to is experimentation on the entity which exists up to the appearance of the so-called primitive streak, at about 14 days. Sometimes this phase is called 'pre-embryonic'.

Degenerative disease: illness that is characterised by progressive deterioration.

Cybrid embryo: a human-animal embryo.

Embryonic stem cell: a primitive kind of cell which goes on to develop into one of the many cells in the body.

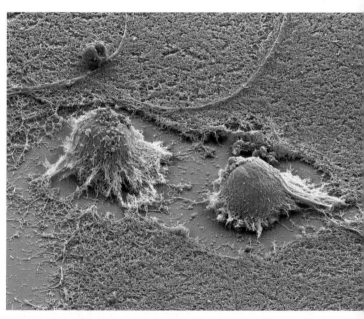

Two embryonic human stem cells. Image created with a scanning electron microscope

■ Activity

The Human Fertilisation and Embryology Authority (HFEA) grants licences for embryo research under the following conditions.

> 'The HFEA cannot grant a licence unless it is satisfied the use of human embryos is necessary or desirable for the purposes of the research and may only be allowed for one of the following purposes:
>
> 1 To promote advances in the treatment of infertility
>
> 2 To increase knowledge about the causes of congenital disease
>
> 3 To increase knowledge about the causes of miscarriages
>
> 4 To develop more effective techniques of contraception
>
> 5 To develop methods for detecting the presence of gene or chromosome abnormalities'

HFEA, 2003

List the purposes given above in order of importance in your view, and decide which if any make a more convincing case for embryo research. Justify your conclusions.

■ Take it further

Use the internet to search for recent reports of medical advances as a result of the use of embryonic stem cell research and adult stem cell research.

Ethical debates about embryo experimentation

The embryo as a potential person

Ethical debates about embryo experimentation start by considering the nature of the embryo; whether it is a person, a potential person or something else, and whether – and to what degree – rights are granted. The argument in favour of embryo research is that before the primitive streak an embryo is not the same as a human person. It has value but not the same value or significance as an older entity. At 14 days old the cells have flattened out to a disc, but the embryo has none of the features we would expect of a human person, a moral being that might make us treat it differently. The embryo at this point has no consciousness and no nervous system.

Peter Singer writes that it is possible to argue that up to 14 days after fertilisation an embryo (as opposed to a foetus) is not a human being because at that time it can split into two or more genetically identical embryos (Singer, 1993, pp156–7). Before 14 days, we cannot be sure if we are looking at one or two individuals, and therefore there is no personal presence. For Singer, this justifies embryo experimentation.

The British Humanist Association agrees with this argument, noting that:

> At the early stage where research is focused, an embryo has few of the characteristics we associate with a person. It is a fertilized human egg, with the capacity to develop into a person, but its cells have not yet begun to form into specialist cells that would form particular parts of the body (which is why they are potentially so useful). There is no brain, no self-awareness (or consciousness), no way of feeling pain or emotion, so an early stage embryo cannot suffer.

British Humanist Association (BHA), 2003

Its use is justified because of a need, possibly to undertake experimentation which cannot be carried out on animal embryos, and more often with a view to making discoveries which will bring about treatments for people who are suffering from terrible diseases and other conditions. It is the combination of these two ethical principles which underpin embryo experimentation: that of the value of the entity before it has the primitive streak, and the uses therefore to which that entity can be put, and also the perceived greater good that will be done for people who suffer terribly now.

The human embryo has clear features that indicate it is an individual being

Others reject the devaluing of the entity prior to 14 days old. They note that even by day seven there are observable features of differentiation:

> The formation of the embryonic disk, and within that disk the epiblast, at about day seven, is a differentiation at least equally significant [as that occurring at about day 14]; in the epiblast are all or virtually all the 'embryo proper' cells. Indeed, the inner cell mass has differentiated from other parts of the embryo by about day five, and functional differentiation of the cells in the embryo begins even earlier ... The fact that some days elapse before one can identify which cells will become placenta and which 'embryo proper' in no way justifies any claim that during those days there is something other than an individual, self-developing human organism, fully continuous with – the very same individual being as – the adult human organism.

Joint Committee on Bioethical Issues of the Catholic Bishops of Great Britain, 1987

Christian absolutists who argue for full rights from the point of conception do not believe that uncertainty about whether it is one or two beings is sufficient to merit the withdrawal of rights from the embryo. Biblical texts such as Jeremiah 1:3, Galatians 1:15, Ephesians 1:4 and Psalm 139 are often quoted to argue that our existence is ordained by God. Any interruption in the process of life interrupts God's plan for life and undermines the idea that God's image is reflected in each human being (Genesis 1:27).

The human embryo is no different than sperm or eggs

The argument, held by some, that an embryo is a potential human being is rejected by Singer, who demonstrates its weakness by extending it to include sperm and eggs. They too could be seen as potential human beings, which simply require a human action for their potential to be realised. He notes that once an embryo is isolated in the laboratory, it too requires a human action for its potential to be realised, and so he does not see that an embryo is very different from sperm or eggs (Singer, 1993, pp158–9). He gives an example of a laboratory assistant who tips some sperm and an egg down a sink and then notices later that the sink is blocked. According to those who argue from the position of potential, the two may well have formed an embryo and so it is wrong to clear the blockage.

Even if the embryo or foetus does not have full human rights, it may have some rights. If it feels pain, then it has an interest in not feeling pain (Singer, 1993, p164), but our knowledge of the activity of the brain in the early embryo and foetus is incomplete – which might, for some, be enough to apply a precautionary rule based on the chance that pain might be caused which we cannot detect.

How we treat imperfect embryos will reflect how we treat imperfect-born humans

However, Richard Doerflinger has argued that:

> That way lies the moral approach of a totalitarian society, that thinks it can use and abuse individual human beings in accordance with some grand scheme promising 'the greatest good for the greatest number'. … If, as modern embryology tells us, … [genetically defective embryos] are indeed part of the continuum of human life, then the notion that genetic flaws enable us to destroy the 'imperfect' embryos has implications for the equal dignity of human beings after birth as well.

Doerflinger, 1997

There are a number of concerns over the use of embryos in research. Should they be used to help develop new treatments for degenerative diseases that harm many people? Does this turn human embryos into a commodity for the greater good of born humans? Should embryos have unique untouchable status irrespective of any benefit that they might give to others through experimentation? The debate over personhood is an important dimension in this discussion, as it is with abortion, and ultimately the view on when an embryo gains rights will heavily influence the ethical position that we take on embryo research. Concerns about the use of one human being for another human being may come from the Kantian principle of treating all people as ends in themselves, a human rights ethic, or a natural law principle to preserve and protect innocent human life. It is conceivable to incorporate a utilitarian perspective into the natural law principle of life preservation, so that very many future lives are protected at the cost of a few lives now, although this would go against traditional formulations of natural law theory. Advocates of embryo research will justify their position on utilitarian grounds, claiming that the betterment of the quality and quantity of human life outweighs the cost of using embryos, which they are unlikely to consider as human beings.

Animal experimentation

- 2.73 million experiments in the 12 months of 2002
- Total number of procedures rose by 4.2% on 2001
- About 80% are for research and drug development
- Safety testing accounts for most of the rest

BBC Science & Nature website

The BBC figures are disputed by animal rights organisations who suggest they do not reflect the whole picture. In the UK, new drugs must be tested on two different species of live mammal, one of which must be a large non-rodent. However, UK law now insists that no animal experiments be conducted if there is a realistic alternative.

One side-effect of having a strict medical regime for the development of drugs is that animals are used for testing. Human life is valued more highly than animal life. The examples at the beginning of this chapter illustrate what can happen if the testing regime is not in place, and the potential dangers of new drugs. The thalidomide tragedy described above led to laws requiring the testing of drugs on pregnant animals. New treatments for new and existing conditions and diseases rely on animal testing. The Royal Society has argued that virtually every medical achievement in the 20th century was possible because animals were used in some way. For many scientists, animal testing and experimentation has been essential in the eradication of disease and alleviation of suffering which we all now depend upon, and it will continue to be essential.

The laws requiring animal testing and experimentation also require consideration of the animals. In Britain an early anti-vivisection movement helped to bring about the Cruelty to Animals Act 1876, which provided some protection to research animals, preventing some major abuses and discouraging some animal experiments. In 1906 a Royal Commission led to the appointment of full-time inspectors as well as a rule requiring the painless killing of animals who suffered severe, enduring pain. Concern in the 1960s and 1970s led eventually to the Animals (Scientific Procedures) Act 1986 which required licences for procedures and inspections.

This raises a number of contentious issues as animals, unlike humans, are unable to give consent. They are treated differently from humans as they are not given the same moral consideration. They are not treated as moral persons, and have far fewer rights than human beings. This becomes particularly contentious when the animals used in testing are primates such as monkeys or apes.

Arguments for and against animal testing

Animal testing has not considered animal welfare

David Degrazia (2002, p98) writes about cat sex experiments carried out for 17 years, beginning in 1960, by scientists at the American Museum of Natural History in New York City. These experiments involved the mutilation of cats in various ways including the removal of parts of their brains and destroying senses of smell or touch by cutting nerves in their sex organs. The scientist then evaluated the cats' sexual performance. This work was funded by the US Government but, Degrazia writes, how this work might have benefited any human being was difficult to fathom. The very idea that it should have led to benefit was queried by the museum's director, Thomas Nicholson, who felt the freedom to experiment was enough. He argued the search for knowledge should never be constrained by concerns for animal well-being. Few of the articles published as a result of these experiments were ever cited in other research.

Other experiments carried out on monkeys seem equally questionable. Infant monkeys were deprived of their mothers at birth and observed to see what would happen. This often produced abnormal behaviour such as self clasping, rocking and convulsive jerking (similar experiments were conducted on human babies by the Nazis). However, in this case the findings were significant. This research led to conclusions that separation from mothers at birth had profoundly negative effects and while this may seem blindingly obvious to us now, it is worth remembering that little more than 30 years ago in Britain, newborn babies were separated from the mothers soon after birth and placed in rooms with all the other newborn babies, only to be brought out to their mothers for feeding. The ethical challenge here is how could conclusions be reached without testing on animals? The kind of testing done on the monkeys sacrifices their interests and well-being for potential benefits to humans.

Animals do not matter as much as humans

Moral philosophers have debated the relative ethical importance of animals as compared to human beings. On the one hand there are those who argue they simply do not have any moral significance, such

■ Link

See Chapter 8 on abortion in *AQA Religious Studies: Ethics AS*.

as Michael A. Fox (1986) who held we have no duty towards them at all. Fox defined members of the moral community as those who could make free rational decisions and were truly persons, and this excluded animals. Although Fox eventually retracted his views others did not, such as Cohan (1998) who only attributes rights to human beings. Like Fox, Cohan thought that animals lacked the basic elements that made human beings moral persons. Human beings are free rational creatures, able to engage with moral dilemmas. Animals have none of these things. Defining personhood is notoriously difficult as several categories of human being do not always show these characteristics, such as newborn babies or those with serious mental disabilities, but we still think it is important to care for these people.

To what extent can humans use animals?

Tom Regan's classic example of the survivors in the lifeboat shows a midway position. He still objects to thinking about animals in terms of things to be used for our pleasure as they have their own lives, even if such lives are different and more limited than ours, although he concedes that ultimately humans are more important.

> [I]magine five survivors are on a lifeboat. Because of limits of size, the boat can only support four. All weigh approximately the same and would take approximately the same amount of space. Four of the five are normal adult human beings. The fifth is a dog. One must be thrown overboard or else all will perish. Whom should it be?
>
> *Regan, 1983*

Regan's view then is that animals have some moral weighting but not quite as much as human beings, while Cohen rejects any moral consideration of animals.

To treat animals differently from humans is 'speciesist'

Peter Singer (1995) takes a stronger position with his argument that all suffering should be given moral significance, even equality, irrespective of the creature that suffers. Treating human suffering as important while at the same time disregarding animal suffering is simply 'speciesist', a form of racism. It is the kind of moral inequality which justified the slave trade and vindicates the poor treatment of women or foreigners or anyone else who seems a bit different. If we are willing to conduct experiments on animals we should be willing to do so on humans. These experiments cause pain and we are happy to cause such pain for food, clothes and experimentation in the case of animals. If we are to be consistent and fair we should do the same to humans or not do it at all, which is Singer's view.

Animal experimentation in balance

The current climate for animal experimentation requires that some benefit might come from experimentation. It may lead to no significant knowledge at all, but that can only be discovered for certain after trying and, historically, advances have been made on the basis of animal experimentation. Degrazia notes that animal testing receives much greater public criticism than factory farming, though morally the potential to do good from medical advances might be stronger than having cheaper food.

Arguments remain about the benefits of animal experimentation. On the one hand advocates suggest that animal studies have helped the development of countless new therapies and techniques. Progress has been made in areas such as Alzheimer's disease, AIDS, cancer, haemophilia, malaria, organ transplantation, etc. Animal medicines and treatments have also been developed. On the other hand opponents argue that such progress could have been made without animal experimentation and there are dangers in using animal experimentation as a guide for humans, as humans are not the same as other animals. It is difficult to judge the likelihood of potential developments. This is an unquantifiable moral variable which complicates the important ethical questions about animal experimentation:

■ Are harmful means justified by good ends? In other words, is the suffering of some animals justified by the good that comes from the discoveries made by study of that suffering?

■ What more significance should be given to animals? Do any animals have similar status to human beings in the moral ballpark? Can animals be used for some human benefits?

Advocates of testing can point to previous examples of developments which have needed such experimentation, but that is only because such experimentation was allowed. The difficulty we have in evaluating these moral arguments is that we live in a moral world where experimentation is permitted; we can only imagine a world where it is not permitted. It is hard to make a decision one way or the other with that uncertainty in mind.

Technological developments

Ethical controls and inventions

> Whether we will acquire the understanding and wisdom necessary to come to grips with the scientific revelations of the 20th century will be the most profound challenge of the 21st.

*Sagan, in **Spier**, 2002*

Human beings have invented and developed extraordinary technologies but they have also demonstrated that they can put such technology to horrific uses. Take for instance the development of Zyclone B gas to make mass extermination much easier (the Nazi Reich found it inefficient to use soldiers to shoot Jews), or the development and dropping of atom bombs after the discovery of how to split the atom. Once a technology becomes theoretically possible, it would seem that human beings inevitably develop and use the technology. Once it became possible to carry out embryo research such research began.

Sometimes science tries to remove ethics entirely, such as attempts to show that all behaviour is determined, and moral action does not exist. E. O. Wilson used neo-Darwinian theory to explain both animal behaviour and human behaviour in his (in)famous book *Sociobiology: The New Synthesis* (1975).

On the other hand there are ethical codes in science which aim to provide some control. In broad terms there are a number of important ethical dimensions of science. When conducting research it is possible for there to be a conflict of interests. A researcher might have a financial interest in a particular company. They might be funded to carry out research to show the particular benefits of a certain product. It is essential that the science determines the result of the research and is not influenced by the generosity of the funding. Scientists can find themselves under enormous pressure from big companies. A bad research report might have

Activities

1 Are harmful means justified by good ends?

2 What moral significance should be given to animals and are some animals more morally significant than others? If so on what basis?

3 'Animal testing is nasty but necessary.' Discuss.

4 'The public are outraged by medical science when it experiments on animals but happy to buy cheap food from factories where animals are treated with cruelty. They are hypocritical.' Discuss.

a harmful effect on the stock value of the company, but false research could endanger lives.

Research institutions have codes of conduct for conflict of interests, and professionals, such as doctors, can be severely reprimanded by their professional organisations if they break the rules. Publication and openness is an important ethical principle in scientific professional ethics. If negative results are hidden then the public standing of science is undermined. How would any privately funded research ever be trusted by the general public if only the positive reports were published? Scientists may also be pressurised to produce results quickly because of the cost of research, which is often very high, and haste can lead to errors. Alvin Weinberg describes the ethical side of science in terms of being a citizen in the 'Republic of Science'.

> Of all the traits which qualify a scientist for citizenship in the republic of science, I would put a sense of responsibility at the very top. A scientist can be brilliant, imaginative, clever with his hands, profound, broad, narrow – but he is not much as a scientist unless he is responsible.

Weinberg, 1978

In addition to the controls of professional ethical responsibilities, there are other ethical audiences. Science takes place in society and therefore some public accountability is important, irrespective of whether the science is funded by the state or private interests. Scientific and technological discoveries can have a huge impact on society at large. Nuclear power may help the world to stop using non-renewable energy resources such as oil and coal, but nuclear weapons have taken their toll on human life, causing political instability and introducing risks to the planet that threaten human civilisation and the survival of the species.

One of the difficulties in establishing ethical controls over science and technology is that, in academic circles, freedom of thought and freedom to research is held highly. If a society exerts too much control over science then developments and discoveries may be lost. In the past religious authorities have exerted pressure on scientists when their findings conflicted with truth as religion perceived it. If I produce research which shows that my religion's creation story is not scientifically true, and everyone in my community believes in that story, am I going to cause instability and anxiety by disseminating my discoveries? At the same time, if it is true then surely I should 'publish and be damned'.

A further problem is that science is a highly complex field that can easily be misunderstood by an ill-educated public. For instance scientists are often asked to say that some drug or procedure cannot do any harm. Scientists prefer to say that they are 99 per cent sure it will not, rather than it cannot. Also, people may react emotively to scientific research and new procedures simply because they are unfamiliar. Some people are very uneasy about the idea of transplantation (having bits of other people inside you or giving bits of yourself to others), but it is an extremely important life-saving area of surgery. Most non-medical professionals would not want to see what goes on in surgery and are quite squeamish in general terms about entirely natural procedures, such as childbirth, undergoing medical checks in 'personal areas', etc. It would be wrong to prevent certain developments due to this sort of squeamishness.

One of the challenges for scientific research is that it is, by definition, trying new things, so there is always a chance that the scientist will go further than the general public is willing to go. Scientists have a responsibility to educate and inform and help the public understand new directions. There must also be recognition by scientists that sometimes, even though we *can* do something, that does not mean we should.

The beneficiaries of scientific and technological advances

Scientific and technological advances in the area of genetic engineering reveal the conflict between ethical principles and the possible beneficiaries of those advances.

What is human cloning?

On 24 February 1997, Ian Wilmot and his fellow scientists at the Roslin Institute near Edinburgh announced to the world that they had cloned a lamb named Dolly. Pictures of Dolly were on the front page of every newspaper in the world. At the time, there was a media frenzy, which quickly turned into panic. Governments took action to prevent the technology being used to clone human beings, but in March 2001 an Italian doctor claimed that he was only months away from starting to clone babies for infertile couples. There are a number of strong medical arguments in favour of the use of cloning technologies, as well as ethical and religious arguments against. Understanding these arguments requires a basic knowledge of the scientific processes involved in cloning.

Cloning is the creation of an embryo using the genetic material from another being. Cloning technology uses embryos because they are a rich source of a special type of cell called a stem cell. Stem cells can replicate themselves and generate more-specialised cell types as they multiply. Stem cells from an embryo are much more versatile than those from an adult.

The procedure works by taking a fertilised ovum (an embryo) with its stem cells, removing the genetic contents of that ovum and replacing them with the genes from another animal. You could take an ovum that has been fertilised by male A and female B. You would then replace the newly created genetic material (combining elements from male A and female B) in that ovum with genetic material from male C. The resulting life would be a genetic copy of male C.

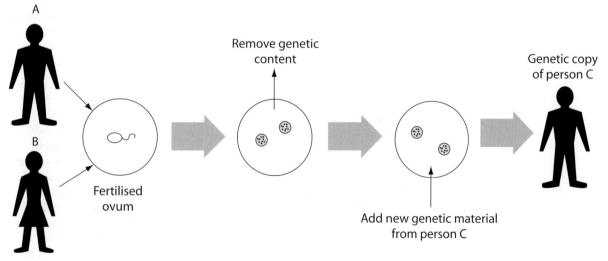

The process of cloning

Therapeutic cloning

There are a number of other possible medical applications using therapeutic cloning in the treatment of degenerative diseases. The human body's specialised cells cannot be replaced by natural processes. Medical conditions that seriously damage them or leave them diseased – such as Alzheimer's disease and Parkinson's disease – are particularly difficult to treat. There is an acute shortage of donated healthy organs, and cloning technology could be used to grow the required cell tissue using stem cells. Once the cells had been grown, they could be injected back into the patient:

> In the long term there could be considerable potential for the use of tissues derived from stem cells in the treatment of a wide range of disorders by replacing cells that have become damaged or diseased. Examples might include the use of insulin-secreting cells for diabetes; nerve cells in stroke or Parkinson's disease; or liver cells to repair a damaged organ … In addition to this potential to develop tissue for use in the repair of failing organs, or for the replacement of diseased or damaged tissues, the technique of cell nuclear replacement might be applied to treat some rare but serious inherited disorders. Repairing a woman's eggs (oocytes) by this technique gives rise to the possibility of helping a woman with mitochondrial damage to give birth to a healthy child which inherits her genes together with those of her partner.
>
> *Department of Health*, 2000

These possible benefits have been used by scientists to encourage the British government to permit research into therapeutic cloning using embryo stem cells, and in 2004 the HFEA issued the first licence to do so. The permit is given with a particular focus on increasing understanding and developing treatments for mitochondrial diseases and it involved stem cells derived from embryonic sources.

Supporters of cloning argue principally for the use of embryos for medical research, on the basis that the results will bring such benefit as to merit the medical process that the embryos have to go through. They maintain that the early embryo is no more than a ball of cells. As it is undeveloped and would not survive outside the womb, research is permissible. The beneficial consequences wholly justify the action. The overall benefits of cloning, the possible treatments that could be made available to sufferers of conditions such as Alzheimer's disease and Parkinson's disease, far outweigh any objections to the use of embryos in experimentation and research. Some Christians have adopted this middle view, which rejects human cloning but allows therapeutic cloning on the basis of the good consequences that it produces. In 1996, the Church of Scotland affirmed the special status of the embryo as created by God, but it also recognised the potential benefits of embryo research under limited circumstances.

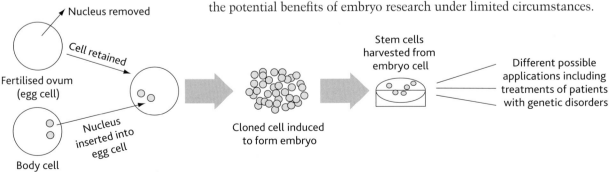

Therapeutic cloning produces stem cells that can develop into different types of body cell

Reproductive human cloning

One possible use of this technology would be for infertile couples who cannot conceive. They could use donor eggs and sperm in order to obtain the necessary embryonic stem cells and then replace the genetic material with (for example) the woman's genetic imprint. The resulting child would be a genetic copy of the mother. Note that, normally, new life has a unique genetic imprint and is made up of elements from both parents. This is not the case in this example. Currently such a practice is prohibited in the UK and some other countries, although if the demand is strong enough it seems likely that it will happen somewhere in the world.

Gregory E. Pence argues that full reproductive human cloning is morally acceptable. In 'Will cloning harm people?' (1998, pp115–28), he states that human cloning would not be harmful as embryos cannot be harmed. While human embryos are lost in the cloning process, this does not harm any person. Pence points out that 40 per cent of human embryos fail to implant in normal sexual reproduction. Thousands of embryos can be stored and many couples decline to pay fees for preserving embryos, hence they are destroyed. Pence is implying that we are using double standards as we are morally concerned by the destruction of frozen embryos while unconcerned with the general loss of embryos as a result of failed implantations. In his view, embryos are not sentient and cannot experience pain. They are not persons and so there is no objection to their use in cloning. Pence believes that the objection to human cloning is an irrational fear of science and things that the general public do not understand.

Identical twins are genetically similar yet distinct individuals

In 'Dolly's fashion and Lois's passion' (1998), Stephen Jay Gould, a Harvard palaeontologist, argues that there are no new ethical questions raised by human cloning. He suggests that identical twins share more properties than Dolly did with her mother. Conjoined twins differ in personalities and achievements, and so human cloning raises no new ethical questions:

> We know that identical twins are distinct individuals, albeit with peculiar and extensive similarities. We give them different names. They encounter divergent experiences and fates. Their lives wander along disparate paths of the world's complex vagaries. They grow up as distinctive and undoubted individuals, yet they stand forth as far better clones than Dolly and her mother.

Gould, 1998

A cloned human being would live in a different time and culture from the source of the gene code. Identical twins are more alike than Dolly and her mother.

In 'Wrongful life, federalism, and procreative liberty' (1998), the law professor John Robertson argues that the use of cloning for reproduction is entirely acceptable:

Activities

1 Why do embryos have to be used for research?

2 Summarise the possible benefits of cloning technology.

If a couple is willing to take the risk that embryos will not form or cleave, that they will not implant, that there will be a high rate of miscarriage, that the child will be born with some defect, and that they will then rear the child, it is hard to see why this is any worse than the other practices that could lead to physically-damaged offspring.

Robertson, 1998

He sees reproductive cloning as another reproductive technology alongside IVF. For some people, it is their only opportunity to have children.

Activities

Read the following extract:

Step forward to a dinner party in 2025. Your hostess warns you that the tomatoes are the new cholesterol reducing ones. Your host grumbles as he eats only organic food. Your gay neighbour tells you how his clone (should you think of it as his son or brother?) is doing at school. Somebody mentions the amount the Smiths have paid to make sure their next daughter has blue eyes. Would not it have been better spent on making her musical? Somebody jokes about the couple who could have had a Margaret Thatcher clone but instead chose a Bill Clinton. On the drive back, the headlines are about attempts to raise the retirement age to 95.

The Economist, *2001*

Identify the different moral issues raised by this extract.

1 Is genetic engineering 'playing at God' or is it exercising morally valid scientific freedom?

2 Should cloning technology be used to determine features of our children?

3 Should the technology be used to help infertile couples reproduce?

4 Would you be happy to have a clone made using your genes?

5 Would you be happy knowing that you were the clone of a parent?

■ Human rights and technology

Introducing human rights

Human rights have a history that dates back to the Stoics' belief in a universal moral law that human conduct can be judged against and brought into harmony with. Later, the Magna Carta (1215) put in place the idea that 'right' was not just what the king did. In England, the Petition of Right 1628 and the Bill of Rights 1689 suggest the view that human beings are endowed with eternal and inalienable rights. In the 17th century, the English philosopher John Locke argued that human individuals have certain rights including the rights to life, liberty and property. The Declaration of Independence, proclaimed by the 13 American Colonies on 4 July 1776, states that 'We hold these truths to be self evident, that all men are created equal, that they are endowed by their Creator with certain unalienable Rights, that among these are Life, Liberty and the Pursuit of Happiness.' This was followed by the Declaration of the Rights of Man (26 August 1789), which defines 'liberty' as including the right to free speech, freedom of association, religious freedom, and freedom from arbitrary arrest and confinement.

With the creation of the Universal Declaration of Human Rights in 1948, a set of principles was established to guarantee equality before the law; protection against arbitrary arrest; the right to a fair trial; freedom from *ex post facto* criminal laws; the right to own property; freedom of thought, conscience and religion; freedom of opinion and expression; and freedom of peaceful assembly and association. The following rights are all included: to work and freely choose one's work; to receive equal pay for equal work; to form and join trade unions; to rest and leisure; to an adequate standard of living; and to education.

The rights expressed in the Universal Declaration take different forms. Some are claims which generate duties that others have. For example, the right to have a loan repaid is a claim that generates a duty to repay the loan. Other rights are powers that we might have in law, such as the right to choose who will inherit your wealth after your death and who cannot. Rights may also be liberties, or freedoms, such as not having to give evidence against your own spouse, or evidence that might prejudice your case in court. Lastly, rights can be immunities, or protections from certain actions, such as violence from another individual, slavery or discrimination due to your political or religious views.

Important in the modern age in addition to the freedoms and liberties discussed above is the right to privacy. It is this right which now seems to be under threat both from growing surveillance and monitoring technologies, and also criminals. A key area of concern in the current age is the protection of individual human rights in a 'surveillance society'. Britain today has more CCTV cameras per head of population than any other country and has the world's biggest DNA database. A number of new ethical questions need to be addressed regarding the use of technologies which might conflict with human rights.

Surveillance

The organisation Liberty is a proponent of human rights. Liberty believes that every individual human life is inherently precious and must be treated with dignity and respect and subject to the values of equal treatment and fairness. Privacy is not absolute because proportionate and lawful intrusion is necessary for things like child protection, tax collection and public safety. But in the introduction to a recent report by Liberty, Gareth Grossman writes:

> Nonetheless, a society which does not pay sufficient regard to personal privacy is one where dignity, intimacy and trust are fatally undermined. What is family life without a little bit of personal space around the home? How do you protect people from degrading treatment (whether in hospital, prison or the home) without paying regard to their privacy? How are fair trials possible without confidential legal advice or free elections without secret ballots? Equally, whilst free speech, law enforcement and public health are often seen in tension with personal privacy, think of anonymous sources, vulnerable witnesses and terrified patients who may be more likely to seek help if their confidences are safe and perceived to be so.

Grossman, 2007

The report explores three different kinds of surveillance: targeted, mass and visual (p2):

■ 'Targeted Surveillance … [is] state sanctioned surveillance against specific targets created under the Regulation of Investigatory Powers Act 2000. It concludes that although the basic structure is sound it lacks accountability and transparency. In particular, there is a need for judicial authorisation for the most intrusive forms of surveillance and an improved complaints mechanism'. The report concludes that surveillance takes place on a massive scale and that 'nearly 440,000 authorisations for communications traffic data took place between June 2005 and March 2006'.

■ Mass surveillance has come about through the huge 'growth and impact of mass databases' and 'the boundary between mass and targeted surveillance is blurring due to the increased use of mass automated processes such as data mining and data matching'. In other words it is becoming easier to trace and track huge numbers of people, searching for evidence of illegal activity among huge innocent populations. CCTV cameras with facial recognition software and number-plate reading software can store movements of civilian population so that simple searches can produce detailed monitoring of ordinary members of the public. Is it acceptable that such data on our movements is stored and accessible by government agencies as a matter of routine?

■ Visual surveillance is the 'Daily exposure to mass CCTV surveillance'. In the UK there are 4.2 million cameras in operation. CCTV can be used for crime detection, but its effectiveness in crime prevention is unknown.

Activities

1 'If you are innocent, you have nothing to hide.' Discuss.

2 To what extent should we be free to go about our affairs without surveillance?

Databases

Our data is found on all sorts of databases. Some doctors' surgeries use databases; schools, hospitals, tax authorities and, of course, banks and credit card companies use them. Shops construct loyalty-card schemes so they can gather enormous amounts of data on buyers and work out what sorts of things they should sell and what sorts of people are coming to their shops. This data reveals valuable information about us which may be used to help teachers plan our next lessons, help doctors understand our medical history and better treat us, and give the government some idea of who is paying their taxes and who is not. On the internet some websites place 'cookies' on our hard drives which monitor where we go after that site. They store information about us so when we return, that data is transferred back to the website that dropped the cookie. It can help retailers to learn about their customers so they can market their products more effectively and produce new products that will appeal to their shoppers. That information is valuable.

Some argue there should be a national DNA database. This would be a complete record of our DNA and would enable police and other public authorities to conduct searches of the data, perhaps finding and convicting criminals who are currently free to commit crimes against members of the public. Currently the UK DNA database has an estimated 3.9 million samples. It is the largest of its kind in the world because under the current law, DNA can be taken and retained following arrest for any recordable offence. According to Liberty this has 'disproportionately affected black men with nearly 40% of black men represented, versus 13% of Asian men and 9% of white men' (Grossman, 2007). DNA is useful in sexual assault or other violent crimes, but should innocent members of the public have their DNA on the database just in case they commit a crime in future? One official has argued that it might be useful if disobedient primary school children were required to give their DNA as they are more likely to commit violent crimes in future so could be caught more easily (Grossman, 2007).

Cyber crime

With the increasing amount of data stored in databases online, with people buying over the internet and banking on the internet, there are serious ethical concerns about growing cyber crime. This includes stealing your banking information, using spyware (software on your computer which monitors your activity and sends information such as passwords to another computer) and identity theft. With identity theft, your personal details are stolen, via the internet, from your computer or from websites and emails. Other sorts of crime are also prevalent on the internet including child pornography and hate websites which target racial or religious groups and advocate or encourage violence towards those groups. The internet is dependent on internet service providers connecting you to the world wide web and also an architecture of computer servers around the world.

Religion, science and technology

Activities

1. Is science heartless?

2. Is religion mindless?

3. Consider the following quotations. Choose one that you find convincing and another that you do not find so convincing and give reasons for your choices.

'A legitimate conflict between science and religion cannot exist. Science without religion is lame, religion without science is blind.'

(Einstein, 1940)

'It is ... idle to pretend, as many do, that there is no contradiction between religion and science. Science contradicts religion as surely as Judaism contradicts Islam – they are absolutely and irresolvably conflicting views. Unless, that is, science is obliged to change its fundamental nature.'

(Appleyard, 1992)

'Science and religion are two windows that people look through, trying to understand the big universe outside, trying to understand why we are here. The two windows give different views, but both look out at the same universe. Both views are one-sided, neither is complete. Both leave out essential features of the real world. And both are worthy of respect.'

(Dyson, Science Spirit website)

'Science can purify religion from error and superstition; religion can purify science from idolatry and false absolutes. Each can draw the other into a wider world, a world in which both can flourish ... We need each other to be what we must be, what we are called to be.'

(Message of his Holiness John Paul II, 1990)

'When religion was strong and science weak, men mistook magic for medicine; now, when science is strong and religion weak, men mistake medicine for magic.'

(Szasz, 1973)

Activities

1. How much is your privacy worth? Is it better to give up our DNA to a central database so that more criminals are caught?

2. Recently a head teacher from a primary school contacted parents to inform them about the new fingerprint-based library system that the school wanted to introduce. The system scans students' fingers when they take out or return books. The school allowed parents to opt their children out of the scheme (the children would get a card instead), but how will those children feel if all their friends go for the fingerprint scanner option when they have a card? Is it unduly technophobic and old fashioned to be concerned, or is there something worrying going on here?

Religion and science in conflict

Religion and science have a troubled history. Richard Blackwell (1999, p11) writes that throughout its long history Christianity has been involved in a love–hate relationship with science. On the one hand there have been times when Christianity has engaged science with great warmth and benefit, as we can see in the synthesis between classical Aristotelian science and Christian theology produced by Thomas Aquinas. Science has also benefited from some religious sources. Blackwell notes that in the 17th century the medieval conviction that the universe is fundamentally rational gave modern science its initial self-confidence. At other times science and religion have opposed each other and a well-known example of this is Galileo's struggles with the Catholic Church and, more recently, the debate over evolution.

Other religions have also had difficulties with science and technology. For instance, while the world of medieval Islam was scientifically more advanced than in the west, in more recent centuries there has been very little interest in scientific developments in some Muslim countries with little money going into scientific research, quite unlike the early history.

There seem to be some tensions and rivalries between science and religion as competing sources of authority. Religion has seemed nervous of scientific discoveries which seem to undermine religious beliefs. At the same time many great scientists held, and still hold, religious beliefs. Not all scientists seek to try to answer religious questions and not all religions try to answer scientific questions, though distinguishing the two might sometimes be difficult.

Religion and technology

Religion has also depended on technological developments and been changed by them. The invention of writing marked a fundamental shift in religious teachings as sacred texts could be written down rather than passed through oral traditions. The printing press meant that religious writings became widely available. Cathedrals and great mosques and temples represent some of the finest achievements in architecture and structural engineering – for instance St Paul's in London or Sulimanye Mosque in Istanbul. In the modern world religions use the internet extensively to propagate beliefs and link communities together.

An important area of conflict in the present age is concerned with medical ethics and, in particular, the use of human embryos. Religions that believe that human life from conception is sacred have great difficulty accepting that embryos can be created for experimentation or for the development of medicines or support of other children. This seems to be using one human person for another. It seems to break a Kantian rule that people should never be treated as means to an end but always ends in themselves, and a religious rule that human life is sacred with a divine purpose or eternal destiny. Scientific breakthroughs may well be made through the use of the human embryo in this way, but religions that regard embryos as having dignity and as being persons, even if only potential persons at that stage, will never be comfortable with it.

Religion and cloning

Cloning is unnatural and against God's will

There are a number of moral dimensions concerning the act of originating a child through cloning. Cloning is opposed on the basis that the act of cloning is intrinsically wrong (a deontological approach) and also because the consequences are harmful. These arguments appeal to God's will or to the unnaturalness of the act. They maintain that from conception onwards the embryo has full human status, thus allowing no research or use that is not to the benefit of the embryo. Any technology that involves the creation of dispensable embryos is rejected. This represents the traditional Christian view which leads Christians to reject abortion, *in vitro* fertilisation and embryo research and experimentation. God creates life, and it is not for humans to destroy even its embryonic form. The former Roman Catholic leader of Scotland, Cardinal Winning, recently said that even though the 'end is good' the 'means are immoral' as they result in the death of 'tiny cloned human beings' (*BBC News Online*, 2000). Dr Michael Jarmulowicz (1999), Honorary Secretary of the Guild of Catholic Doctors, notes that it has always been accepted in British law that the earliest human embryo should be treated with respect and accorded a special status. He argues that to use the human embryo for basic science research that has not yet been undertaken in animals would end the special status that embryos deserve. He also maintains that therapeutic cloning could become possible from adult cells in the future, which would save the lives of the embryos used in the research and, finally, that to allow therapeutic cloning would invariably lead to human cloning.

Cloning could harm society

Cloning is also rejected because of the harmful impact that it might have on human society, the family or the child. These consequentialist objections identify harm that might be done to the individual being cloned and to society as a whole. Leon Kass opposes cloning in his article 'The wisdom of repugnance' (1998). He sees the common repugnance that people express towards cloning as a revolt against the excess of human wilfulness and a warning not to do something that is profoundly unspeakable. It is a sign that human nature no longer commands respect. In his article, Kass goes on to state that:

- Human cloning will harm the created child by threatening a confusion of identity and individuality because, 'She is the work not of nature or nature's God but of man, an Englishman' (pp13–14).
- Because the cloned person will be in genotype and appearance identical to another human being, possibly a parent, the child will have a crisis of identity (p27).

Cloning turns reproduction into manufacturing

Human cloning represents a step towards turning reproduction into manufacturing: 'if sex has no intrinsic connection to generating babies, babies need have no necessary connection to sex' (Kass, 1998, p16). In natural sexual reproduction, each child has two complementary biological progenitors. Cloning turns begetting into making. Procreation becomes manufacture, which makes man another part of man-made things. In natural procreation, human beings come together, complementarily male and female, to give existence to another being who is formed. A cloned human being is a product of intention and design (pp29–30).

Finally, Kass argues that cloning represents a form of despotism of the cloners over the cloned, and represents a blatant violation of the inner meaning of parent–child relationships. A child stems from and unites two lineages. The exact genetic constitution is decided by nature and chance, not human design. He believes that these biological truths express truths about our identity and our human condition. Reproduction that does not involve sex is not natural and rejects common family relations (pp30–1).

Donald Bruce (2000), director of the Church of Scotland's Society, Religion and Technology project, rejects not only human cloning but also the use of cloned embryos for therapeutic cloning:

> It is my view the creation and use of cloned embryos for procedures such as these should not be allowed ... I believe we should stop in our tracks, and not continue to use embryos routinely for cell therapy.

Bruce, 2000

He argues that it is not consistent to allow an embryo to be created but then prevent it from coming to full term. It is wrong to create an embryo as a resource for others. It should be afforded dignity in itself. Bruce also voices concern about 'ethical gradualism' – allowing far-reaching ethical processes by a series of small steps, the first of which is therapeutic cloning.

Consequential and deontological views of cloning

If the cloning debate is addressed in terms of its consequences, the resulting good must be balanced against the resulting bad. Childless couples seeking children would have the potential to have children. Those suffering from a variety of terrible degenerative diseases might have the chance of a cure. But these goods must be weighed against the potential bad. The cloned individual might be psychologically or emotionally damaged. There may be erosion in society's attitude to life and reproduction. The technology could be used by those with dubious motives.

A deontological approach looks to the rightness or wrongness of the action in itself. If the embryo has full human status from conception, then embryo research and human cloning is immoral because a number of embryos would die. To create life in an asexual way is unnatural: it attacks the dignity of sexuality and therefore human dignity. The nature of the ethical debate will depend upon whether the proponents take deontological or teleological approaches. It will be subject to the proponents' fears about what will happen if either therapeutic or reproductive cloning comes about. It would appear that soon we are going to find out what the consequences are. Therapeutic cloning is already taking place in the USA, and it may only be a short time before reproductive human cloning is a reality.

■ Issues arising

Should science be controlled by ethics?

Two fundamentally opposing ethical viewpoints clash when we try to control science by ethics (or to guide science by ethical considerations alone). On the one hand there are deontological absolutists who hold up the dignity of every human person and never allow that to be compromised for any greater good. On the other hand utilitarianism argues for the greatest good for the greatest number. Sometimes, harm

Activities

1 What links the Roman Catholic Church's criticism of human cloning with that of IVF, abortion and embryo research?

2 What other specifically religious reasons are there for opposing human cloning?

3 How might human cloning change our understanding of sex and, in your view, would this be a positive or negative development?

4 What possible harms might human cloning cause to the individual?

5 What possible harms might human cloning cause to society?

6 How might it be argued that a clone raises no more ethical questions than an identical twin?

7 Outline the argument for a person's right to clone.

must be risked for one in order for others to benefit, as is the case with human testing.

Beyond these ethical theories which conflict with medical experimentation in particular, there are also professional ethical issues. Here the question of the public trust which people have in the authorities, the scientific community, the armed forces and so on is important. Certain processes may be ethically permissible but publicly unpopular. Here there is a case for the public to be educated.

An uneducated or untrusting public can be harmful, as is the case of the children who were not vaccinated during the MMR scare (when dubious scientific research was blown out of proportion by the media, scaring parents about the safety of a vaccination). In some areas there is now considerable risk to children who were not vaccinated against serious illnesses because parents were scared of trusting the advice of the medical authorities. Here the issue and importance of public trust in professional ethics is illustrated. Bad journalism and bad medical research undermined public health.

There must be a balance between the expertise of scientists, who may have a clearer perspective than the less-informed public, and the ethical principles of society. Such a balance is challenging in a diverse and plural society where there are competing values. This might be thought of as respectful decision making. Respect can be given to dissenting voices, and conversation should be allowed to help society develop in a way which shows an awareness of its religious and ethical traditions, as well as scientific and technological changes.

How should ethics respond to new scientific ideas?

Because of the unpredictability of scientific discoveries, it is hard to imagine how ethics could do anything other than respond to new situations as they emerge. Ethics always seems to be in a situation where it has to catch up and try to hold back developments which are taking place continuously. This way of thinking separates ethics from the science. We think of some ethical committee outside science chastising scientists for creating Frankenstein's monster. These moral experts control what is done or not done. That idea is rather removed from the truth. There are countries where religious leaders have considerable influence outside the official systems of government (such as the Catholic Church in Ireland and Poland, for instance, and its influence on reproductive technologies and genetic engineering). There are also countries where religious leaders have more direct control over medical research, as in the case of Iran. However, in more secular liberal democracies, the government, Parliament, advisory groups made up of different interest groups and pressure groups all have ethical agendas. Ethics is not a single entity but is distributed across religious and other interest groups, political groups and professional groups.

Perhaps a better way is to see ethics as part of the scientific community. Scientists need to think ethically. They have professional ethical responsibilities, both in terms of how they go about their research and also in terms of how they communicate to non-specialists in the wider world. This is especially the case in new technologies as the public are often nervous and ill-informed about the current state of affairs in the world of medical science let alone the future. All areas of life need strong professional ethical codes of conduct and behaviour. There may still be clashes with other interest groups with different ethical standards and principles, but at least there can be a dialogue between scientists and others about those ethical codes and principles.

Can a scientific discovery be 'undiscovered'?

It could be argued that once we *can* clone human beings, someone somewhere in the world *will* clone them. Once a thing becomes possible, it is done. Once we were able to split the atom, we made atomic bombs and dropped them. Opponents of new technologies argue that they should be abandoned. So, for instance, all nuclear weapons should be dismantled or cloning prohibited. However, once knowledge exists, perhaps human beings will always find a way of testing it out. Arguably, the only difference is that the benefits of the technological developments will be privately owned by the company which developed them and not as available to the scientific community in more regulated countries. In fact they may be misused as they will have been developed in an unregulated environment.

As in the case of nuclear weapons, it has been argued that once invented a country should try to acquire them in order to protect itself from the other countries which already have them. They cannot be uninvented. Even if every country destroyed their nuclear weapons, the knowledge would still exist for a rich terrorist to build one and then hold the world to ransom. Arguably, it is better that new technologies are allowed to be developed and are controlled in a regulated environment agreed by the international community.

Perhaps multimillionaires will be able to go to some independent island for genetic improvement treatments, essentially giving technological benefits to the rich and powerful. If this was to happen, there could be a divide between the 'super haves' and the 'have nots' as rich people evolved in new ways while poorer ones did not. The dilemma facing governments is this: if they do not allow technological developments, will those developments simply become secret operations undertaken by the rich?

How far should society allow religion to control scientific and technological development?

Scientific and technological development takes place within research establishments which may by state-funded (usually universities) or privately funded bodies (a research and development part of a company). In the UK, government regulation controls the deployment of new technologies so, for instance, drug regulatory authorities license new medicines for specific uses. In the British parliamentary democracy new technologies and scientific developments are controlled ultimately by an elected Parliament which can be voted out during general elections. Government-appointed bodies, such as the HFEA, may have representation from religious and other interested communities to help guide decision making. However, even though there is an established Church of England, religions do not have ethical controls over science and technology, Parliament does. Of course research establishments have ethical processes for their research activities and companies may also have such guidelines, but these are self-regulatory processes.

Tensions emerge in society where particular groups differ from the perceived consensus. For instance, in the case of embryo experimentation, some religious groups object to the use of embryos for experimentation. They do not necessarily want to stop developments, but they do try to influence the way developments take place so that, for instance, the individual dignity and sanctity of the human person are taken into account. In other countries, such as Iran, religious authorities have direct powers to prevent or allow development and practices.

To what extent should religion have any special position in influencing laws beyond the usual democratic process? Does it represent an important tradition of thought that should have a special voice of authority on matters of public importance? The same questions can apply to any pressure group seeking to change the law on an issue it feels to be important. Governments are aware of public opinion (they cannot survive elections without public support). They listen to pressure groups and other interest groups (including religious groups) to form a view on what society's values are and how they apply to particular issues. However, the public may express morals that religions disagree with, or they may express naïve views about science and technology which frustrate developments. Society may have muddled values, as suggested by the observation that while lots of people do not like the idea of animal testing, they are happy to eat factory produced chickens. This can make things difficult for the scientific community who, by their nature, are seeking to make new discoveries and develop new technologies.

Extracts from key texts

Albert Einstein

Scientific statements of facts and relations, indeed, cannot produce derivatives. However, ethical derivatives can be made rational and coherent by logical thinking and empirical knowledge. If we can agree on some fundamental ethical propositions, then other ethical propositions can be derived from them, provided that the original premises are stated with sufficient precision. Such ethical premises play a similar role in ethics to that played by axioms in mathematics.

*Einstein, 1940, in **Frank**, 1950*

Mary Wollstonecraft Shelley

When I found so astonishing a power placed within my hands, I hesitated a long time concerning the manner in which I should employ it. Although I possessed the capacity of bestowing animation, yet to prepare a frame for the reception of it, with all its intricacies of fibres, muscles, and veins, still remained a work of inconceivable difficulty and labour. I doubted at first whether I should attempt the creation of a being like myself, or one of simpler organisation; but my imagination was too much exalted by my first success to permit me to doubt of my ability to give life to an animal as complex and wonderful as man. The materials at present within my command hardly appeared adequate to so arduous an undertaking; but I doubted not that I should ultimately succeed. I prepared myself for a multitude of reverses; my operations might be incessantly baffled, and at last my work be imperfect: yet, when I considered the improvement which every day takes place in science and mechanics, I was encouraged to hope my present attempts would at least lay the foundations of future success. Nor could I consider the magnitude and complexity of my plan as any argument of its impracticability. It was with these feelings that I began the creation of a human being. As the minuteness of the parts formed a great hindrance to my speed, I resolved, contrary to my first intention, to make the being of a gigantic stature; that is to say, about eight feet in height, and proportionably large. After having formed this determination, and having spent some months in successfully collecting and arranging my materials, I began.

***Shelley** (1818), Frankenstein, 1961*

Jeremy Bentham

The day may come when the rest of the animal creation may acquire those rights which never could have been withholden from them but by the hand of tyranny. The French have already discovered that the blackness of the skin is no reason why a human being should be abandoned without redress to the caprice of a tormentor. It may one day come to be recognized that the number of the legs, the villosity of the skin, or the termination of the os sacrum are reasons equally insufficient for abandoning a sensitive being to the same fate. What else is it that should trace the insuperable line? Is it the faculty of reason, or perhaps the faculty of discourse? But a full-grown horse or dog is beyond comparison a more rational, as well as a more conversable animal, than an infant of a day or a week, or even a month, old. But suppose they were otherwise, what would it avail? The question is not, Can they reason? nor Can they talk? but Can they suffer?

Bentham (1789), 2005, Chapter 1

Peter Singer

If a being suffers there can be no moral justification for refusing to take that suffering into consideration. No matter what the nature of the being, the principle of equality requires that its suffering be counted equally with the like suffering – in so far as rough comparisons can be made – of any other being. If a being is not capable of suffering, or of experiencing enjoyment or happiness, there is nothing to be taken into account. So the limit of sentience (using the term as a convenient if not strictly accurate shorthand for the capacity to suffer and/or experience enjoyment) is the only defensible boundary of concern for the interests of others. To mark this boundary by some other characteristic like intelligence or rationality would be to mark it in an arbitrary manner. Why not choose some other characteristic, like skin colour?

The racist violates the principle of equality by giving greater weight to the interests of members of his own race when there is a clash between their interests and the interests of those of another race. The sexist violates the principle of equality by favoring the interests of his own sex. Similarly the speciesist allows the interests of his own species to over ride the greater interests of members of other species. The pattern is identical in each case.

How can a man who is not a sadist spend his working day heating an unanesthetized dog to death, or driving a monkey into a lifelong depression, and then remove his white coat, wash his hands, and go home to dinner with his wife and children? How can taxpayers allow their money to be used to support experiments of this kind? And how can students go through a turbulent era of protest against injustice, discrimination, and oppression of all kinds, no matter how far from home, while ignoring the cruelties that are being carried out on their own campuses?

The animal liberation movement … is not saying that all lives are of equal worth or that all interests of humans and other animals are to be given equal weight, no matter what those interests may be. It is saying that where animals and humans have similar interests – we might take the interest in avoiding physical pain as an example, for it is an interest that humans clearly share with other animals

– those interests are to be counted equally, with no automatic discount just because one of the beings is not human. A simple point, no doubt, but nevertheless part of a far reaching ethical revolution.

Singer, 1985

■ Chapter summary

Human and animal experimentation

- Medical breakthroughs have saved many lives.

- Mistakes with drug treatments have taken lives, such as the thalidomide tragedy.

- Animal and human testing is part of the process by which drugs are given licences to be sold.

- Ethical issues include the responsibility of researchers, scientists and doctors, and the practice of pharmaceutical companies.

- The state has a duty to protect civilians from the dangers of the unregulated development and use of drugs.

- Informed consent is important for human experimentation, though sometimes life-saving treatment requires attempts using untried procedures.

- Embryo experimentation is advocated for some because of the potential it has to offer cures for some terrible illnesses. This is justified on 'greatest good' grounds.

- Opponents are concerned that the embryo could be a person or potential person and deserves respect.

- Supporters such as Singer and the BHA claim that in the first 14 days the embryo has so few of the characteristics that we would recognise as human that it should not be treated as a human being, though opponents reject this.

- Christian absolutists identify conception as the start of the human person.

- Ethical concerns also include the idea that embryos are a commodity to be used to help others, rather than treating them as ends in themselves.

- Animal testing is also required in the development of some drugs, including species closer to human beings such as primates, but some of this testing has been for no obvious gain and has caused great suffering in the animals.

- On the other hand, unpleasant testing has revealed important truths about the importance of some of our practices, such as keeping newborn babies with mothers.

- Michael Fox initially argued that animals are not members of the moral community so can be used for our benefit, but then he changed his mind.

- Singer argues that animals have a degree of equality with human beings, so they should not suffer.

- Advocates argue that animal experimentation has helped to bring about many benefits.

Ethical controls and inventions

■ Human beings have developed technologies and used them to commit horrendous acts on fellow human beings.

■ Science has ethical codes to maintain responsible conduct on matters of openness and where there are conflict-of-interest related issues.

■ Society is affected by scientific and technological developments and so the relationship between the values of society and science is important.

■ Scientists need to have a degree of freedom to pursue research, they should not be restricted by over-anxious non-specialists.

The beneficiaries of scientific and technological advances

■ Ethical conflicts emerge between principles and the possible beneficiaries of advances.

■ In the case of genetic engineering this includes couples who cannot conceive and those suffering from degenerative diseases.

■ Some are concerned about possible psychological damage for the children of this new science, others think the concerns reflect a lack of understanding.

Human rights and technology

■ Human rights grant freedoms including the right to life, liberty, property and also privacy.

■ In the UK there are many CCTV cameras and other methods of tracking the movement of innocent people, with the aim of preventing criminals or catching them after they have committed a crime.

■ Liberty has concerns that the new technologies are being used without enough judicial oversight and that the use of mass surveillance means that a lot of information about innocent people is stored for possible use in catching criminals.

■ In addition the development of databases with enormous amounts of information storing detailed data about shopping preferences, finances, medical information and possible biometric data raises new concerns about the loss of privacy for the innocent in the interest of catching the guilty.

Religion, science and technology

■ Some argue that religion holds back science, while others say that science needs religion to keep it on the straight and narrow.

■ Historically Christianity has restricted some scientific developments at some times, while it has utilised science in other ways in other eras.

■ Religion and science can be seen as rival sources of authority.

■ Religion is particularly concerned with the treatment of very early human beings (embryos).

■ Many religions are opposed to cloning because a good end is not justified by a bad means, namely the destruction of a human embryo.

■ Cloning seems to distort the normal parent–child relationships.

■ Further reading and weblinks

There has been an explosion in publishing in this field as fast-moving developments leave publishers trying to catch up.

Grossman, G. (ed.) *Overlooked: Surveillance and Personal Privacy in Britain*, Liberty, 2007, www.liberty-human-rights.org.uk/issues/3-privacy/pdfs/liberty-privacy-report.pdf. This presents a recent survey of concerns about the erosion of individual freedoms in a surveillance society by the campaigning organisation dedicated to the protection of civil liberties.

Light, A. and Rolston III, H. *Environmental Ethics, An Anthology*, Blackwell, 2007. A terrific collection of some 40 essays in seven parts with good part introductions.

Lovelock, J. *The Revenge of Gaia*, Allen Lane, 2006. This is a recent update of James Lovelock's original thesis. It is concise and very readable.

Wilmot, I. and Highfield, R. *After Dolly: The Uses and Misuses of Cloning*, Little Brown, 2006. A treatment of some of the ethical issues joint authored by one of the scientists responsible for the Dolly breakthrough.

In this chapter you have:

- explored a number of important issues relating to science, technology and ethics
- examined ethical arguments for and against human, embryo and animal experimentation
- considered different arguments regarding the question of ethical controls, the beneficiaries of technological breakthroughs, aspects of human rights and surveillance, data storage and cyber crime
- considered different aspects of the relationship between religion and science.

AQA Examination-style questions

Chapter 1 Libertarianism, free-will and determinism

1   (a) Examine the view that humans act freely because of a combination of their
          genes and their environment.   *(30 marks)*

     (b) Assess the claim that humans are not free to act and make choices.   *(20 marks)*

Chapter 2 Virtue ethics

2   (a) Explain Aristotle's view of virtue ethics, and show how this view can be
          applied to one ethical issue you have studied.   *(30 marks)*

     (b) Evaluate the argument that Virtue Ethics is of little value as an ethical system.   *(20 marks)*

Chapter 3 Religious views on sexual behaviour and human relationships

3   (a) Examine one religious view of the concept of love.   *(30 marks)*

     (b) Assess how far religious views on love are relevant to people today.   *(20 marks)*

Chapter 4 Science and technology

4   (a) Explain what one religion you have studied teaches about inventions and the
          way their uses should be controlled.   *(30 marks)*

     (b) Discuss how far society should allow religion to control scientific and
          technological developments.   *(20 marks)*

Glossary

A

Ascetic tradition: describes a lifestyle characterised by abstinence from various sorts of worldly pleasures.

C

Causally undetermined: when a moral choice is made, there is no overriding power making the person choose one or another.

Conjugal: married lovemaking.

Cosmopolitan: accepting of groups and individuals from different cultural, ethnic and religious backgrounds within society.

Covenantal group: a group bound by a covenant with God.

Cybrid embryo: a human-animal embryo.

D

Dalits: sometimes called the untouchables, the lowest level of the Indian caste system.

Degenerative disease: illness that is characterised by progressive deterioration.

Dualism: the division of the world between the physical and the spiritual.

E

Embryo experimentation: a term that can cause confusion. For the sake of this chapter, what is being referred to is experimentation on the entity which exists up to the appearance of the so-called primitive streak, at about 14 days. Sometimes this phase is called 'pre-embryonic'.

Embryonic stem cell: a primitive kind of cell which goes on to develop into one of the many cells in the body.

Eudaimonia: (as defined by Aristotle) what makes a person truly happy.

Excessive or deficient: having too much or too little of a characteristic, e.g. rashness and cowardice for the virtue courage.

G

Golden mean or virtuous mean: the midway point between the vices of excess and deficiency.

H

Hard determinists: those who maintain that all human actions are effects, caused by prior influences.

I

Incompatibilitists: people who hold the view that free will is incompatible with determinism. Those with the view that free will is compatible with determinism are called compatibilists.

L

Libertarians: those who maintain that we are free to act and morally responsible for those actions.

P

Patriarchal views: views that are related to or characteristic of a system of society controlled by men.

Phocomelia: a deformity whereby the individual has very short or absent limbs.

Predestination: the view that God has already decided who will be saved and who will not.

S

Sacrament: traditionally, an outward sign of inward grace ordained by God.

Sages: wise people.

Sangha: the monastic community of ordained Buddhist monks or nuns.

Sati: the immolation of a widow on her husband's funeral pyre.

Soft determinists: those who maintain that some human actions are determined, but that we still have moral responsibility.

Stoics: a group of Greek philosophers who regarded with disapproval the sense of loss of control and animal instinct involved in sexual excitement.

Supreme happiness: the end to which virtue theory looks, an end which is both about an individual person's development and the whole community.

T

Thalidomide: a drug prescribed from 1957 to 1961 in many countries chiefly to pregnant women to combat morning sickness.

U

Unitative: the uniting aspect of sex.

Bibliography and websites

Abu Hamid al-Ghazali, ihya ulum al din ('Revivification of the Religious Sciences') (Cairo n.d.), 27, cited in Fatima Mernissi, *Beyond the Veil: Male-Female Dynamics in Modern Muslim Society* (rev. edn Al Saqi Books, 1985) 29

Ādi Granth, the Holy Scripture of the Sikhs, 1469–1708

Annas, J. 'Ancient ethics and modern morality', in Childress, J. F. and Macquarrie, J. (eds) *Philosophical Perspectives, 6: Ethics* SCM, 1992

Anscombe, E. 'Modern moral philosophy', *Philosophy*, 1958, 33: 124, January. See www.philosophy.uncc.edu/mleldrid/cmt/mmp.html

Appleyard, B. *Understanding the Present – Science and the Soul of Modern Man*, Pan Books, 1992

Aquinas, St Thomas (1274) *Summa Theologica*, trans. by the Fathers of the English Dominican Province, Benziger Bros, 1947

Aristotle (350 BCE) *The Nicomachean Ethics*, trans. with an introduction by W. D. Ross, Oxford University Press, 1980

Augustine, St, Bishop of Hippo, 'De Trinitate', in *William of Auvergne, The Trinity, of the first principle* (De Trinitate, Seu De Primo Principio), Medieval Philosophical Texts in Translation, No. 28, Marquette University Press, 1984

Augustine, St, Bishop of Hippo, Sermon 26, xii, 13; in Migne, J. P., *Patrologia Latina*, 38:177A–B

Ayer, A. J. *Philosophical Essays*, Macmillan, 1954

BBC News Online, 'Churchman attacks cloning as "immoral"', 27 November 2000. See http://news.bbc.co.uk/hi/english/uk/scotland/newsid_1042000/1042869.stm

BBC Science and Nature, 'Hot topics, animal experiments'. See www.bbc.co.uk/ethics/animals/using/facts.shtml

Belliotti, R. 'Sex', in Singer, P. (ed.) *A Companion to Ethics*, Blackwell, 1991, pp315–26

Bentham, J. (1789) *An Introduction to the Principles of Morals and Legislation*, Clarendon Press, 2005

Bible, *The New Jerusalem Bible*, Darton, Longman and Todd, 1990, Romans 2:15

Blackwell, R. J. *Science, Religion and Authority: lessons from the Galileo Affair*, Marquette University Press, 1999

Boswell, J. *Rediscovering Gay History: archetypes of gay love in Christian history*, Gay Christian Movement, 1982

Bowie, R.A. *Ethical Studies*, Nelson Thornes, 2001, p136

Bowker, J. *Worlds of Faith*, BBC/Ariel, 1983

Brijbhushan, J. *Muslim Women: in purdah and out of it*, Vikas Publishing House, 1980, p56

British Humanist Association, 'A humanist way of … embryo research', 2003. See www.humanism.org.uk/site/cms/contentViewArticle.asp?article=1230

Bruce, D. *The Tablet*, 26 August 2000, p1127

Buddhist Publication Society, *Everyman's Ethics: four discourses by the Buddha (WH14)*, trans. by Thera, N., Buddhist Publication Society, 1985

Butler, J. (1726) *Fifteen Sermons*, Bell, London, 1964

Calvin, J. (1559) *Institutes of the Christian Religion*, in McNeill, J. T. (ed.), trans. by Battles, F. L., Westminster Press, John Knox Press and SCM Press, 1960

Campbell, C. A. 'On selfhood and Godhead' in Minton, A. (ed.) *Philosophy: paradox and discovery*, McGraw-Hill, 1976

Church of England, *Marriage and the Church's Task (the Lichfield Report)*, CIO Publishing, 1978

Cohan, C. 'The case for the use of animals in biomedical research' in Cahn, S. M. and Markie, P. (eds) *Ethics, History, Theory and Contemporary Writings*, Oxford University Press, 1998, pp829–37

Cole, W. Owen, *Six World Faiths*, Continuum, 2004

Congregation for the Doctrine of the Faith, *Persona Humana*, Continuum, 1975

Crisp, R. and Slote, M. *Virtue Ethics*, Oxford University Press, 1997, p26

Crook, R. H. *An Introduction to Christian Ethics*, Prentice Hall, 2002

Daley, M. *Beyond God the Father: toward a philosophy of women's liberation*, Beacon, 1973

Daly, M. 'The qualitative leap beyond patriarchal religion', *Quest*, 1974, 1, 32–43

Degrazia, D. *Animal Rights: a very short introduction*, Oxford University Press, 2002

Department of Health, *Stem Cell Research: medical progress with responsibility*, DOH, June 2000, pp6–7

Doerflinger, R. 'Forbidden knowledge: a discussion of the federal ban on human embryo research', 14 March 1997. See www.pbs.org/newshour/forum/march97/embryo2.html

Dominion, J. *Passionate and Compassionate Love. A Vision for Christian Marriage*, Darton, Longman and Todd, 1991

Dyson, F. Science & Spirit website. See www.science-spirit.org/printerfriendly.php?article_id=201

Einstein, A. 'On Science and Religion', *Nature*, 1940, p146

Flannery, A. (general ed.) *Dignitatis Humanea, the Declaration on Religious Liberty* in *Vatican Council II, Constitutions, Decrees, Declarations*, Dominican Publishing Translation, 1996, pp551–68

Foot, P. *Virtues and Vices*, Clarendon Press, 2002

Fox, M. A. *The Case for Animal Experimentation: an evolutionary and ethical perspective*. University of California Press, 1986

Frank, P. *Relativity – A Richer Truth*, Beacon Press, 1950

Fromm, E. *Man for Himself*, Holt, Rinehart and Winston, 1947

Frymer-Kensky, T. 'Law and philosophy: the case of sex in the Bible', in Magonet, J. (ed.) *Jewish Explorations of Sexuality*, Berghahn Books, 1995

Gaither, C. C. *Scientifically Speaking: a dictionary of quotations*, CRC Press, 2000

Gaudium et spes (Pastoral Constitution), in Flannery, A., (general ed.) *Vatican Council II, Constitutions, Decrees, Declarations*, Dominican Publishing Translation, 1996

Geaves, R. 'Islam and conscience', in Hoose, J. (ed.) *Conscience in World Religions*, Gracewing, 1999, pp154–7

Gorsky, J. 'Conscience in the Jewish tradition', in Hoose, J. (ed.) *Conscience in World Religions*, Gracewing, 1999 pp129–54

Gould, S. J. 'Dolly's fashion and Lois's passion', in Pence, G. (ed.) *Flesh of my Flesh: the ethics of cloning humans*, Rowman & Littlefield, 1998, pp101–10

Gragam, L. R. *Between Science and Values*, Columbia University Press, 1981

Greenberg, B. 'Female sexuality and bodily functions in the Jewish tradition', in Becher, J. (ed.) *Women, Religion and Sexuality: studies on the impact of religious teachings on women*, Trinity Press, 1991, pp1–44

Grossman, G. (ed.) *Overlooked: surveillance and personal privacy in Britain*, Liberty, 2007, pii. See www.liberty-human-rights.org.uk/issues/3-privacy/pdfs/liberty-privacy-report.pdf

Gruen, L. 'Animals', in Singer, P. (ed.) *A Companion to Ethics*, Blackwell, 1991, pp343–53

Hampson, D. *Theology and Feminism*, Blackwell, 1990

Harvey, P. *An Introduction to Buddhist Ethics: foundations, values and issues*, Cambridge University Press, 2000

Hassan, R. 'An Islamic perspective', in *Women, Religion and Sexuality: studies on the impact of religious teachings on women*, Trinity Press, 1991, pp93–115

Hekmat, A. *Women and the Koran: the status of women in Islam*, Prometheus Books, 1997

HFEA (Human Fertilisation and Embryology Authority), 'Human embryo research', 2003. See www.hfea.gov.uk/en/372.html

Honderich, T. (ed.) *The Oxford Companion to Philosophy*, Oxford University Press, 1995

Honderich, T. *How Free are You? The determinist problem*, Oxford University Press, 2002

Hoose, B. (ed.) *Christian Ethics, an Introduction*, Cassell, 1998

Hume, D. (1748) 'An enquiry concerning human understanding', in *Enquiries Concerning Human Understanding and Concerning the Principles of Morals*, Clarendon Press, 1975

James, W. *The Dilemma of Determinism*, Kessinger Publishing, 2005. See http://csunx2.bsc.edu/bmyers/WJ1.htm

Jarmulowicz, M. Hon. Secretary of Guild of Catholic Doctors, Comments to the Chief Medical Officer's Expert Group on Cloning, 29 October 1999

Jerome, St, in Potts, T. *Conscience in Medieval Philosophy*, Cambridge University Press, 2002

Johnston, J. *Lesbian Nation: the feminist solution*, Simon and Schuster, 1974

Joint Committee on Bioethical Issues of the Catholic Bishops of Great Britain 1987, statement responding to recommendations of the British government's Warnock Committee, 9 July 1987. See *Origins* 17: 144–7, 30 July 1987

Kane, R. (ed.) 'Free will: new directions for an ancient problem' in *Free Will*, Blackwell, 2003

Kant, E. (1785) *Foundations of the Metaphysics of Morals*, trans. by Paton, H. J., Routledge, 1948

Kass, L. 'The wisdom of repugnance', in Pence, G. (ed.) *Flesh of my Flesh: the ethics of cloning humans*, Rowman & Littlefield, 1998, pp13–38

Keenan, J. F. 'Virtue ethics', in Hoose, B. (ed.) *Christian Ethics, an Introduction*, Cassell, 1998 pp84–94. See also *Dialogue, a Journal for Religious Studies and Philosophy*, 15 November 2000

Keown, D., *Buddhist Ethics: a very short introduction*, Oxford University Press, 2005

Khayyam, O. (1120) The Rubiyat in the entry 'Determinism' in *Encyclopedia Britannica*, copyright 1994–99

Knott, K. *Hinduism: a very short introduction*, Oxford University Press, 2000

Laplace, P. (1820) 'Essai Philosophique sur les Probabilités', in *Théorie Analytique des Probabilités*, V. Courcier; reprinted in Truscott, F. W. and Emory, F. L. (trans.), *A Philosophical Essay on Probabilities*, Dover, 1951

Locke, J. (1690) in Beauchamp, T. L. (ed.) *An Enquiry Concerning Human Understanding*, Oxford University Press, 2006

Louden, R. 'On some vices of virtue ethics', in Crisp, R. and Slote, M. (eds) *Virtue Ethics*, Oxford University Press, 1997, chapter 10

MacIntyre, A. *A Short History of Ethics*, 2nd edn, Taylor and Francis, 1966

MacIntyre, A. *After Virtue: a study in moral theory*, 2nd edn, University of Notre Dame Press, 1985

MacKinnon, C. A. *Feminism Unmodified: discourses on life and law*, Harvard University Press, 1987

Mansukhani, G. S. *Introduction to Sikhism*, Hemkunt Press, 1986

Martin Soskice, J. 'Can a feminist call God "Father"?' in Kimel, A. F. (ed.) *Speaking the Christian God: the Holy Trinity and the challenge of feminism*, Gracewing, 1998

McGrath, A. *Christian Theology, An Introduction*, Blackwell, 1994

McKenna, M. 'Compatibilism' entry, *The Stanford Encyclopedia of Philosophy*, first published 26 April 2004. See www.science.uva.nl/~seop/entries/compatibilism/#3

Medical News Today 'Stem cell treatment improves mobility after spinal cord injury', 11 May 2005. See www.medicalnewstoday.com

Mernissi, F. *Women and Islam*, Blackwell, 1991

Message of his Holiness John Paul II, in Russell, R. J. Stoeger, W. R. and Coyne, G. V. (eds) *John Paul II on Science and Religion: reflections of the new view from Rome*, Vatican observatory, 1990, pM13

Metro 'Blind stem cell "cure" in 5 years', 5 June 2007

Mill, J. S. (1859) *On Liberty and the Subjection of Women*, Wordsworth Classics, 1996

Moore, G. *The Body in Context: sex and Catholicism*, SCM, 1992

Moore, G. 'Interpersonal and sexual ethics', in Hoose, B. (ed.) *Christian Ethics, an Introduction*, Cassell, 1998, pp223–47

Morgan, P. and Lawton, C. *Ethical Issues in Six Religious Traditions*, Edinburgh University Press, 1996

Morton, A. *Philosophy in Practice*, Blackwell, 1996

New International Bible, copyright 1973, 1978, 1984 by the International Bible Society

Pence, G. E. 'Will cloning harm people?', in Pence, G. E. (ed.) *Flesh of my Flesh: the ethics of cloning humans*, Rowman & Littlefield, 1998, pp115–28

Peters, T. 'Playing God?', *Genetic Determinism and Human Freedom*, Routledge, 1997

Plaskow, J. *Standing Again at Sinai*, Harper One, 1991

Porcile-Santisco, M. 'Roman Catholic teachings on female sexuality', in *Women, Religion and Sexuality: studies on the impact of religious teachings on women*, Trinity Press, 1991

Potts, T. C. *Conscience in Medieval Philosophy*, Cambridge University Press, 1980, p10

Qur'an, the central religious text of Islam

Rachels, J. *Elements of Moral Philosophy*, McGraw-Hill, 1986

Radcliffe, T. 'The joy of giving ourselves', *The Tablet*, 23 February 2008, pp12–13

Radford Ruether, R. 'Catholicism, women, body and sexuality: a response' in *Women, Religion and Sexuality: studies on the impact of religious teachings on women*, Trinity Press, 1991, pp221–32

Regan, T. *The case for animal rights*, University Presses of California, 1983

Regan, T. 'The case for animal rights', in Singer, P. (ed.) *In Defence of Animals*, Blackwell, 1985

Religious Tolerance website, www.religioustolerance.org

Robertson, J. 'Wrongful life, federalism, and procreative liberty', in Pence, G. (ed.) *Flesh of my Flesh: the ethics of cloning humans*, Rowman & Littlefield, 1998

Rockman, H. 'Sexual behaviour among ultra orthodox Jews: a review of laws and guidelines', in Magonet, J. (ed.) *Jewish Explorations of Sexuality*, Berghahn Books, 1995, pp191–205

Roman Catholic Church, *Catechism of the Catholic Church*, Pope John Paul II, Geoffrey Chapman, 1994

Romans 8:28–30, New International Version

Russell, B. 'The science to save us from science', *The New York Times Magazine*, 19 March 1950

Ruthven, M. *Islam: a very short introduction*, Oxford University Press, 2000

Sagan, C. *Billions and Billions: thoughts on life and death at the brink of the millennium*, Random House, 1997

Saunders, K. and Stamford, P. *Catholics and Sex*, Heinemann, 1992

Schaller, W. 'Are virtues no more than dispositions to obey moral rules?', *Philosophy*, 1990, 20 (July), 1–2

Shattuck, C. *Hinduism*, Routledge, 1999

Shelley, M. *Frankenstein: or, the modern Prometheus*, Collier Books, 1961

Singer, P. *Practical Ethics*, Cambridge University Press, 1993

Singer, P. *Animal Liberation*, Pimlico, 1975, 1995

Singer, P. (ed.) *In Defence of Animals*, Blackwell, 1985

Solomon, N. *Judaism: a very short introduction*, Oxford University Press, 2000

Southern Baptist Convention, 'The Family: Baptist faith and message', 2000

Spier, R. E. *Science and Technology Ethics*, Routledge: 2002

Spinoza, B. (1674) 'A study of the ethics of Spinoza', in Joachim, H. H. (ed.) *Ethica Ordine Geometrico Demonstrata*, Oxford Clarendon Press, 1901

Stackman, E. 'US science holds its biggest powwow', in *Life*, 9 January 1950

Starn, R. *Ambrogio Lorenzetti: The Palazzo Pubblico, Siene*, George Braziller, 1994

Sviri, S. 'The song of songs: Eros and the mystical quest', in Magonet, J. (ed.) *Jewish Explorations of Sexuality*, Berghahn Books, 1995

Szasz, T. *Science and Scientism, The Second Sin*, Anchor/Doubleday, 1973

Thatcher, A., *Living Together and Christian Ethics*, Cambridge University Press, 2002

The Bible, Revised Standard version

The Economist, 'Perfect?' 12 April 2001, p15

United Methodist Church, *Book of Discipline*, United Methodist Publishing House, 1996

Urban, H. B. *Sex, Secrecy, Politics, and Power in the Study of Religion*, University of California Press, 2003

Voltaire (1764) *Dictionaire Philosophique*, selected and translated by Woolf, H. I., Knopf, 1924

Waskow, A. 'Down-to-earth Judaism: sexuality', in Magonet, J. (ed.) *Jewish Explorations of Sexuality*, Berghahn Books, 1995, pp221–36

Weinberg, A. M. 'The obligations of Citizenship in the Republic of Science', in *Minerva*, 1978, 16, 1–3

Wilson, E. O. *Sociobiology: the new synthesis*, Harvard University Press, 1975

Young, R. 'The implications of determinism', in Singer, P. (ed.) *A Companion to Ethics*, Blackwell, 1997

Index